Surveillance: A Very Short Introduction

VERY SHORT INTRODUCTIONS are for anyone wanting a stimulating and accessible way into a new subject. They are written by experts, and have been translated into more than 45 different languages.

The series began in 1995, and now covers a wide variety of topics in every discipline. The VSI library currently contains over 750 volumes—a Very Short Introduction to everything from Psychology and Philosophy of Science to American History and Relativity—and continues to grow in every subject area.

Very Short Introductions available now:

ABOLITIONISM Richard S. Newman
THE ABRAHAMIC RELIGIONS
    Charles L. Cohen
ACCOUNTING Christopher Nobes
ADDICTION Keith Humphreys
ADOLESCENCE Peter K. Smith
THEODOR W. ADORNO
    Andrew Bowie
ADVERTISING Winston Fletcher
AERIAL WARFARE Frank Ledwidge
AESTHETICS Bence Nanay
AFRICAN AMERICAN HISTORY
    Jonathan Scott Holloway
AFRICAN AMERICAN RELIGION
    Eddie S. Glaude Jr.
AFRICAN HISTORY John Parker and
    Richard Rathbone
AFRICAN POLITICS Ian Taylor
AFRICAN RELIGIONS
    Jacob K. Olupona
AGEING Nancy A. Pachana
AGNOSTICISM Robin Le Poidevin
AGRICULTURE Paul Brassley and
    Richard Soffe
ALEXANDER THE GREAT
    Hugh Bowden
ALGEBRA Peter M. Higgins
AMERICAN BUSINESS HISTORY
    Walter A. Friedman
AMERICAN CULTURAL HISTORY
    Eric Avila
AMERICAN FOREIGN RELATIONS
    Andrew Preston
AMERICAN HISTORY Paul S. Boyer

AMERICAN IMMIGRATION
    David A. Gerber
AMERICAN INTELLECTUAL
    HISTORY
    Jennifer Ratner-Rosenhagen
THE AMERICAN JUDICIAL SYSTEM
    Charles L. Zelden
AMERICAN LEGAL HISTORY
    G. Edward White
AMERICAN MILITARY HISTORY
    Joseph T. Glatthaar
AMERICAN NAVAL HISTORY
    Craig L. Symonds
AMERICAN POETRY David Caplan
AMERICAN POLITICAL HISTORY
    Donald Critchlow
AMERICAN POLITICAL PARTIES
    AND ELECTIONS L. Sandy Maisel
AMERICAN POLITICS
    Richard M. Valelly
THE AMERICAN PRESIDENCY
    Charles O. Jones
THE AMERICAN REVOLUTION
    Robert J. Allison
AMERICAN SLAVERY
    Heather Andrea Williams
THE AMERICAN SOUTH
    Charles Reagan Wilson
THE AMERICAN WEST
    Stephen Aron
AMERICAN WOMEN'S HISTORY
    Susan Ware
AMPHIBIANS T. S. Kemp
ANAESTHESIA Aidan O'Donnell

Available soon:

For more information visit our website

www.oup.com/vsi/

David Lyon

SURVEILLANCE

A Very Short Introduction

OXFORD
UNIVERSITY PRESS

Great Clarendon Street, Oxford, OX2 6DP,
United Kingdom

Oxford University Press is a department of the University of Oxford.
It furthers the University's objective of excellence in research, scholarship,
and education by publishing worldwide. Oxford is a registered trade mark of
Oxford University Press in the UK and in certain other countries

Published in the United States of America by Oxford University Press
198 Madison Avenue, New York, NY 10016, United States of America

British Library Cataloguing in Publication Data
Data available

Library of Congress Control Number: 2023946355

ISBN 978-0-19-879684-8

Printed and bound by
CPI Group (UK) Ltd, Croydon, CR0 4YY

Links to third party websites are provided by Oxford in good faith and
for information only. Oxford disclaims any responsibility for the materials
contained in any third party website referenced in this work.

Contents

Acknowledgements

I gratefully acknowledge the kind and patient help of several readers whose wise and pertinent comments and suggestions helped me to improve this book: Azadeh Akbari, Mark Andrejevic, Kirstie Ball, Didier Bigo, Sara Degli-Esposti, Pablo Esteban Rodríguez, Rafael Evangelista, Rodrigo Firmino, Pete Fussey, Ariane Ollier-Malaterre, Lucas Melgaçao, Aaron Martin, David Murakami Wood, Mike Nellis, Midori Ogasawara, Christina Pilgrim, Priscilla Regan, Sachil Singh, Emily Smith, Katarzyna Szymielewicz, Kristin Veel, and Dean Wilson. Thanks to Jolyon Mitchell for encouraging me to write this VSI. I alone take responsibility for the final version. At Oxford, Andrea Keegan, Jenny Nugee, Luciana O'Flaherty, and Imogene Haslam have been supportive, long-suffering, and accommodating. The support of Sue, my life-partner, continues strong. I'll thank her personally.

List of illustrations

Chapter 1
Living with surveillance

Surveillance is everywhere and always-on. Cameras watch you on the highway, in the shopping mall, and on the bus. More personally, your phone allows companies to track you as you move from one environment to another. In many workplaces your employer knows exactly what you are doing and how well you are performing at any given moment. Others may know how well you are in health terms. During the COVID-19 global pandemic, many countries enhanced their public health data systems to try to track and slow the infection rates. Conducted appropriately, along with adequate testing, treatment, and care, such surveillance can save lives. Surveillance is part of everyday existence.

For instance, few householders realize the contribution they make to wastewater surveillance. The pandemic prompted authorities to upgrade their routine testing of domestic sewage, which contains revealing genetic matter. Successive waves of COVID-19 are often recognized first—before contact-tracing—by this method. Such data enable health professionals shape their advice to ordinary citizens, about wearing masks, being vaccinated, or when indoor activities can recommence. Public health departments can tell, rapidly, where the virus is heading before people show symptoms. But as with all surveillance, the genuine human benefits have to be weighed carefully against possible disadvantages. Vulnerable populations, such as minority groups, may not be fairly served by wastewater testing, and poorer countries may be unable to afford it, for example.

Surveillance today depends on many kinds of data, not least from social media. Such data are used for consumer advertising, and also by public health and security agencies. Many police departments take advantage of personal data from the 'open source' of social media to check what's happening at key moments or sites, whether urban crime 'hotspots' or airports, seaports, or train stations. At the same time, of course, social media platforms also allow us to watch each other, while health and fitness apps let us watch ourselves.

Unless they were wanted criminals, had overstayed their visa, (in some cases) were black or gay, or were suspected spies or inattentive workers, your grandparents were unlikely to have any such sustained contact with surveillance when they were young. And when they did, it was intermittent, contained within the organization, and, except with difficulty, could not be checked with other agencies. Surveillance was a word associated with person-to-person spying or police special agents, not an everyday reality or something we might engage with ourselves. It was simply not on the radar of daily life and didn't have the advantages of today's technology.

Surprisingly, perhaps, considering how completely surveillance has enveloped our lives in the 21st century, few people know much about it, except in a vague way. Do we, for instance, have any idea where our data goes when it leaves our phones and laptops, how we might benefit from it, who has access to it, who wishes to use it and for what purpose? We might be pleased that big stores know our preferences and make special effort to inform us when targeted special offers are available. We might worry about 'privacy' or even 'identity theft', but who knows what other tangible harms might occur as a result of our data being used, misused, or abused by companies or government departments?

And do we know how to judge if an apparent trade-off—privacy for security or convenience, for example—is worthwhile or even safe? Do we even know that there may be a trade-off?

This book gives some context for exploring these issues. Today, surveillance has become an unprecedentedly central, pervasive, but largely unseen feature of society. Our lives have become increasingly visible to others who take a deliberate and systematic interest in their details. But those others are less and less visible to the people whose details are being collected, analysed, and acted upon. We may be aware of surveillance, but our awareness of its extent is limited. Also, surveillance activities have to be recognized in many contexts where they might not at first be expected.

Take, for example, browsing the internet when suddenly you notice an advertisement appear in a sidebar and a flicker of recognition occurs. A company you've never heard of is trying to sell you exactly the kind of running shoes you looked up yesterday, when you wanted to know about the best brands for trail use. Or you think your WhatsApp conversation produces ads on Facebook (now part of the umbrella company Meta). Clearly, your activities may be visible and audible to companies, but who are they, and how did they find their way to your phone or laptop? For some, this experience feels creepy, but to others, commonplace and unremarkable.

The sense that someone is targeting you may seem unnerving because it is the result of surveillance. Someone has access to the details of your spending habits, conversations, and other personal details, and they are using these to try to sell you something. You may want to give this activity a name other than 'surveillance'. Maybe 'marketing' would be better? Well, yes, that could work. But marketers still seek details of your spending habits, your identification data, your everyday contacts, your preferences and commitments, and your location and movements, so that they can inform you, and nudge and prod you towards certain products and purchases for profit.

Such activities may not be seen as surveillance, not least because the surveillance aspects are not always obvious. The academic Shoshana Zuboff uses a revealing term—surveillance capitalism—that indicates how central surveillance has become to the economic and political systems that surround us today. Surveillance capitalism's raw materials are the details of our everyday lives, harvested from our online lives. Probing this phenomenon is woven into this book's fabric (and elaborated in Chapter 7).

So it's important to recognize that seemingly trivial surveillance is bound up with the very ways that society is organized, to provide for and protect us, and also with how power operates, and how our everyday opportunities and choices are shaped and channelled.

What is happening in the world of surveillance?

Most significantly, surveillance is growing exponentially in the 21st century. What may be less than obvious, however, is just how much data is gathered on each of us, constantly. Boosted by the pandemic, in every minute in 2022, says the 'Data never sleeps' website, Instagram users shared 66,000 photos, users uploaded 500 hours of YouTube videos, WhatsApp users shared 41,666,667 messages, Facebook users shared 1.7 million pieces of content, Snapchat users sent 2.43 million snaps, and 104,600 hours were spent in Zoom meetings. Not to mention WeChat, Weibo, Baidu, and other major Chinese platforms. Data from these are all recorded, the raw material of much surveillance. Assuredly, these figures will have mushroomed by the time you read this book. And the environmental consequences of such growth are also huge. By 2015, the datacentres that power all kinds of digital services were responsible for 2 per cent of greenhouse gas emissions, on a par with the aviation industry.

That growth goes with other important trends listed here: 'security' is a major driver of surveillance, from local to global levels. Public and private surveillance agencies are increasingly intertwined, so it is hard to know where one ends and the other begins. What counts as 'private information' is increasingly hard to define. Mobile and location surveillance is expanding, so that *where* you are at a given moment is often known and acted upon. Surveillance practices and processes are becoming globalized, even planetary. With the advent of the so-called Internet of Things, surveillance is embedded in everyday environments such as homes, buildings, and vehicles. Surveillance often depends on data taken from our bodies by biometric technologies such as body scanners or voiceprint recognition. We interact more than ever with surveillance using platforms of the sharing economy and social media. Mutual surveillance—or 'social surveillance'—using social media is growing, constantly.

Three key issues run through this book. One, surveillance is an ambivalent practice. It offers great potential for human flourishing, as much can be discovered about how today's world works by scrutinizing the data produced by human presence and activities. At the same time, surveillance practices are always uncertain because they may not adequately portray persons or populations fairly or appropriately. Surveillance inevitably has ethics and politics.

Thus, two, persons deserve to be respected as such, which may give rise to concerns about privacy and related claims, such as 'data justice'. And three, as groups in the population are often consequentially classified using surveillance, we focus on processes of 'social sorting' to grasp how surveillance works. Simply put, data are used to distinguish between one group and another, so that the groups can be treated differently. In the public health example above, groups in certain geographical areas can benefit from early warnings from wastewater data. But because the techniques and technologies of surveillance are always sensitive, their origins and basic impulses have to be transparent. Surveillance makes us visible in particular ways, which is then how we are represented and treated. To seek privacy and data justice is to find fair ways of revealing, characterizing, and dealing with people.

Chapter 2
Visible lives: invisible watchers

What is surveillance?

A dictionary might say 'surveillance is close observation, especially of a suspect or criminal'. But while surveillance includes such activity, this definition is much too specific and limited for today's digital world. At its simplest, surveillance is any attempt to find out about people in order to influence or manage them. More fully, surveillance is any routine, focused, and systematic attention to personal details for purposes such as influence, management, protection, and control.

However, these definitions describe surveillance from an 'operator' perspective. We could also say that surveillance is the operation *and experience* of the collection, analysis, and use of personal data to shape choices or administer groups and populations. The experience of being surveilled may be positive, when being watched by others is sought for the pleasure of performance. Many social media *afficionados* long to be looked at or even followed by others as a means of acquiring status. But it may also raise negative emotions if it is felt, for instance, that surveillance is intrusive or a tool for enforced conformity.

Surveillance is about watching, as the word itself indicates. *Surveillance* is a French word meaning 'watching over'. It may be direct watching, as a police officer might watch a suspect on the street or a lifeguard a swimmer in the waves or even a video camera installed at traffic lights. But it may also be datafied—tracking travellers by their data trail or, in political scientist James Scott's words, as 'seeing like a state'. This means making citizens visible in particular ways—through, say, tax-paying or household data from a census—so that their activities can be monitored and managed.

Indeed, while the word 'surveillance' is rooted in watching and visibility, from early times it appeared in other modes. Think of eavesdropping or checking written records, or even more obscurely, checking wastewater. Surveillance embraces a wide range of modes for making people and their activities 'visible' or for bringing them to the attention of others. Here, we use 'surveillance' in an inclusive manner, including in its toolbox everything from fingerprints to voiceprints, from facial recognition systems to online location tracking and beyond. Surveillance is decidedly multimodal.

This book, then, is about visibility in a broad sense. Just as a state 'sees' citizens, visibility is about how people are seen and how they respond to being seen and recorded—and also, by extension, how they are *not* seen and remain invisible. Surveillance in the most obvious sense makes people visible to organizations; corporations, healthcare agencies, police, welfare workers, for example, that wish to entice, support, regulate, direct, shape, or otherwise intervene in their activities. But this is not necessarily directly apparent to people seen by these organizations, and thus it is ambiguous. You may or may not wish to be seen.

To some, surveillance seems negative, perhaps sly, secretive, and even sinister. Whether it is tiny surveillance drones or insects, the interception of mobile phone communication, or even, from earlier times, eyes behind window curtains and keyholes—think Shakespeare's play *Hamlet*, where much watching is surreptitious—surveillance seems to be about being seen by unseen watchers. Even if what is 'seen' is in the form of digital data and is not literally visible. We often appear to have little choice about how we are seen, and assessed, through our data. Police, government departments, employers, marketing companies, or intelligence agencies are all able to see us without our seeing them or knowing in what ways they are watching us.

This is why considering not only the *operation* but also the *experiences* of surveillance is significant. Increasingly, it is taken for granted that surveillance of all kinds is going on. This may just be everyday surveillance, for instance as we are geolocated and tracked on our daily commute, by traffic engineers using anonymized data, or through transit cards in the subway.

Or it may have to do with concerns about terrorism and public safety, especially since the attacks on New York and Washington on 9/11, and, subsequently, from Mumbai in 2008 to Myanmar in 2021.

We may well experience surveillance as helpful and constructive, convinced that body-worn cameras on police officers help to ensure that justice will be seen to be done, or that cameras mounted above traffic lights will limit accidents from drivers running red lights. Many are reassured to know that both checked and carry-on bags are X-rayed at the airport, because such systems are calibrated to detect potentially hazardous items such as guns or bombs. And it is useful for cities to know that today's city subway payment systems—debit cards, smartphone apps, or loadable cards—ensure that everyone has paid appropriately for their ride.

Such reassuring aspects of everyday surveillance should not be discounted. Police ought to be accountable for their actions, and drivers for their behaviour at traffic lights. Anxious air passengers should be able to relax, knowing that bags are checked for safety, and underground commuters should know that a uniform system collects their fares. Many would agree that these are desirable dimensions of daily life, and that some such systems are needed to ensure public order, safety, and fairness.

At the same time, such systems also demand public debate about surveillance. Does using a subway smartphone app mean other data are collected for purposes unknown to us? How efficient are the X-ray machines and CT scanners in airports? Is 'humanitarian' border surveillance being used to keep certain nationalities out of a country? Does the level of accident reduction justify the installation of red light cameras? Will data from body-worn cameras be acceptable in a law court? There are undoubted benefits from many surveillance systems, but the systems are complex and many legitimate questions arise as soon as any new surveillance system—whether seen as 'surveillance' or not—is announced or installed.

On one hand, surveillance may be seen as an intrusion on our private lives, or as a brake on our freedom to think, say, or do things that we believe to be our own business—unless of course we have actually broken a law. Many understand this as a violation of privacy, whether involving our space, inside our homes, for instance, or our bodies, challenged by the use of our DNA or biometrics, or by images, whether photos or fingerprints. Or we may think of privacy as guarding words we don't want others to hear or communications and other personal activities over which we wish to retain control.

No doubt you have heard people affirm that certain kinds of surveillance are acceptable to them. A common phrase is 'I have nothing to hide and nothing to fear,' which in an ideal world would ring true. The idea might be plausible if it were not for social sorting. As we have already seen, this often has benefits in the public health sphere. In other contexts, from policing to banking, surveillance tries to distinguish between those who are or are not 'suspect', 'lazy', 'credit risks', 'untrustworthy', and so on. Placing persons in categories allows one to organize what is 'seen' so that different groups may be treated according to their category, rather than by traits or behaviours peculiar to them. Today such processes are automated.

As communications scholar Oscar Gandy shows in his book *The Panoptic Sort: A Political Economy of Personal Information* (2021), the more such categorial distinctions are made to appear 'scientific' the more valid they seem. As he summarizes elsewhere, statistical discrimination

> …occurs when an employer refuses to hire an African American male because he is assumed to be ignorant, dishonest, lazy or criminally-inclined on the basis of generally-held and perhaps statistically-validated [through inaccurate data], estimates of the distribution of those traits among African Americans.

Thus, what might otherwise be seen as illegal racial, discrimination is 'scientifically' justified as legitimate and rational. When decisions are being made on the basis of data that you are unaware is being collected by opaque systems, the discrimination is harder to detect. You may have nothing to hide but still have something to fear or that will at least make you cautious. This is discussed more fully in Chapter 6.

Data analysis vastly expands such techniques and now, massive amounts of available data, plus machine learning and Artificial Intelligence (AI) mean that classification is carried out by sophisticated algorithms. For instance, facial recognition involves complex technology, and companies—not without controversy— use millions of images scraped from social media to offer their services to police and others to help trace wanted or missing individuals.

Credit scoring provides further examples of computerized surveillance, as does smart or 'predictive' policing (discussed further in Chapter 4). Add to this the ways that social media platforms have built-in methods for ranking and rating performances and personalities, and it becomes clear that such social sorting is not only complex in operation but also consequential—for better or for worse—in outcomes for those classified.

Nearly 6 billion people are active online globally, the world's security agencies work together in global partnerships, and government administration runs on data amassed for multiple purposes, so surveillance is clearly not just an individual matter. Surveillance today is a global if not a planetary issue, something human beings now experience and encounter in common. Our apparently private worries are actually shared, in different ways, on a large and public scale. So surveillance is a social, ethical, political, and economic issue; perhaps even a cultural, aesthetic, and spiritual one. When this is understood and acted on, it may help to produce shared strategies and solutions for confronting its difficulties and dilemmas.

Surveillance today is easily misunderstood. The word often conjures up visions of powerful agencies keeping an unwelcome watch over us, intruding on our privacy and restricting our freedoms. Ask most people and they will say that surveillance is a negative word. It recalls George Orwell's Big Brother (Figure 1), or a real-life dictator, breathing down our necks, making us feel nervous, anxious, threatened by forces we fear as much for their mysterious as for their menacing aspects. But it doesn't necessarily have to be this way.

Surveillance: a complex story

Surveillance has antique roots, whether in *ch'a-kuan* officials administering China's Shang dynasty almost 3,000 years ago or

1. The 'telescreen' in the 1956 British film *1984*.

Greek military espionage under Alexander the Great. The Hebrew scriptures note how watchers stand guard at the city gate or on the city wall, scanning for danger, monitoring movement, warning of attack, theft, or unusual behaviour. The Christian New Testament tells of Jesus' parents, obliged by an imperial Roman census to return to their hometown of Bethlehem to be enumerated.

It was not until about the 16th century that surveillance began to affect people in more routine ways. Increasing population mobility from the 17th century in Europe, for example, prompted concerns about who had responsibility for the poor, producing investigations and interventions. More generally, as sociologist Georg Simmel observed, the figure of the stranger becomes more significant. Trust was challenged as, proportionately, face-to-face relationships gradually gave way to more fleeting encounters. Tokens of trust were needed, which by the 20th century appeared in the form of identification: drivers' licences, credit cards, and passports. These then became the basis for citizenship claims.

13

City growth also spawned new kinds of policing, not to mention the use of planning and architecture to maintain maximum visibility. Paris was named the 'city of light' not for tourists but for Jean-Baptiste Colbert's street lighting scheme in the 1660s. Just over 100 years later, in the 1790s, another design innovation was to have a lasting effect on prisons. English social reformer Jeremy Bentham, keen to reform austere and brutal places of punishment, sketched a prison diagram (Figure 2) that would in effect require inmates to discipline themselves.

The 'Panopticon', indicating an 'all-seeing place', was a multi-storey prison design, whose circular plan involved central 'inspection'.

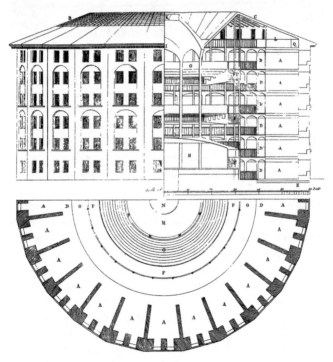

2. Jeremy Bentham's Panopticon design.

However, prisoners were prevented from knowing when they were watched by blinds that hid the inspector from sight. The inspector had the advantage of seeing without being seen, thus obliging inmates to watch themselves, as it were, checking that they were observing the rules and fulfilling the expectations of the institution. The philosopher Michel Foucault later pinpointed the Panopticon as a pivot on which modern surveillance turned. A fascinating thought, but one open to many questions.

In this 'all-seeing place', Foucault averred, 'visibility became a trap'. It was intended to automate control, dispensing entirely with physical violence and relying instead on the prisoner's own self-discipline, fabricated from fear of the consequences of non-compliance. In this sense, the surveillance was *formative*, in that those subject to the hidden gaze would be reformed as reliable citizens. Foucault contends that, when the threat of physical punishment is discarded, people discipline themselves, through situations created to foster the fear of being seen. This was also the supervisor's dream of complete control.

However, while the 'visibility' aspect of the Panopticon plays a significant part in understanding surveillance, this is by no means the whole story. Bentham's plan was formative, a way of ordering social relationships, not merely a vision machine. It was a social and physical device for sorting and arranging categories of groups and individuals so that they could be seen in particular ways. The 'inspector' sorted prisoners into groups depending on their crimes or their risk of violence, which may be seen as a way of managing populations through classification, or social sorting. They were thus evaluated for their appropriate place in the social system. Bentham thought of his Panopticon as a model for other institutions from the factory to the school or hospital.

Interestingly, when discussing the Panopticon, Foucault observed that its principles could be seen on a larger scale during the 17th-century plagues in Europe. People were told to stay home and constant inspections took place so that governing bodies could control the chaos, bringing order and discipline to society. Techniques for registering victims and measuring and limiting the spread of the plagues, hints Foucault, were the embryonic surveillance of the modern age. Those who lived through Ebola, SARS, and then the COVID-19 pandemic may not be aware of the longer history of surveillance in mitigating 'plagues'.

Surveillance was also a by-product of introducing more 'scientific' approaches to life. As military personnel were professionalized, for instance, drills were developed to calculate each move for greater efficiency. In expanding cities, policing for social order kept track of offenders through more sophisticated watching. Government administration was bureaucratically organized using ordered files and official hierarchy, facilitating surveillance of both things and people.

One of the most pervasive forms of surveillance may be seen in welfare states in the later 20th century. To avoid a repeat of the miserable inter-war depressions, in Europe and the USA, national systems were created, intended to ensure that neither unemployment, old age, nor illness would mean a slide into poverty and deprivation. But some means of tracking the population was required, so people were numbered for 'National Insurance' (UK) or 'Social Security' (USA). Such numbering is basic to welfare surveillance.

In this case, the purpose of surveillance was socially positive and gratefully received by millions. Welfare states made people feel recognized, and mitigated fears that some citizens had about being known by a number. Such risks were taken in the belief that large-scale provision of benefits required large-scale bureaucratic handling. The need for registration, evaluation, and appropriate distribution was paramount and this served to obscure some potentially negative surveillance dimensions of welfare states, until computerization and the additional uses of the numbering system—needed, for instance, to obtain a US driver's licence—started to ring warning bells.

That pattern, of military, policing, welfare, and business interests escalating surveillance, has not diminished in the 21st century. However, the mushrooming of technology in all these areas, along with new pressures of political economy—such as greater government–business collaboration—have also contributed profoundly to the ways that surveillance has developed. During the 20th century, the rise of authoritarian states, the consequences of colonization, and the Cold War, all made their mark on surveillance practices.

Once limited to specific silos like government or business, surveillance is now a basic feature of the digital world, fed by data from many sources, that flow within and between organizations of many kinds.

Features of surveillance today

The first feature is that surveillance is something that happens continuously, within many agencies and organizations. It is not simply a single event triggered by a suspicion about a possible offender or an eager click on a page of the internet. This is because organizations harvest massive amounts of data in the hope that patterns of consumption or movement or relationship will reveal something about you that is financially worth tracking and monitoring because it is a source of economic value.

Many American shopping malls, for example, have smart digital camera systems that follow your movements—by which door you entered, which vendors you visit, and so on—to check on your spending habits and to try to shape your future shopping experience. This could be thought of as 'seeing like a market'. But most surveillance today operates beyond such bricks-and-mortar settings. For example, cars have become a key site for electronic gadgets, all of which collect data about the operation of the vehicle, but also about its driver and other users. Such data are very valuable to the automobile industry and often contribute to road safety as well.

Secondly, surveillance is increasingly automated. In most cases, no human being decided that you are a target. These systems are created to make you visible to the organization or platform whenever you send a message, cross a threshold, complete an action, or appear somewhere. Such visibility is specific to the purpose of the surveillance. Decades ago, when computers were introduced to help manage factory production or office work, automated ways of organizing staff became popular, at least among managers. But it was not just a matter of computers taking on new tasks, previously done by people; those computers kept records which had the effect of making all aspects of the workplace more visible.

Workplace processes were, as social psychologist Shoshana Zuboff observed, 'informated' rather than merely automated. New *sorts* of information—styles of working, lengths of breaks, and so on—became available to managers *along with* automation, which improved their ability to surveil and helped to redistribute authority upwards.

At the same time, something similar was happening in policing, where surveillance was commonplace. Sociologist Gary T. Marx, who argues consistently for the beneficial aspects of some surveillance, warned in the 1980s that the growing dependence of police on computers raised the prospect of a broader 'maximum security society' where computerized records increased the transparency of everyone. He insisted that this was occurring inside the 'industrial democracy' of the USA.

A third feature of surveillance today is that it is embedded in the routines and the environments of everyday life. This is a far cry from the secret agent, hat down and collar raised, slinking through the shadows, trailing a suspect down city streets. Those streets now have their own cameras and sensors, just as buildings keep track of their occupants, cars monitor their drivers—sometimes preventing them from driving if they have had too much to drink—and phones keep a continuous record of where, when, how, and by whom they are used. Scanners, detectors, and recording devices are part of daily life, offering convenience, safety, or reassurance but also, simultaneously, silently surveilling.

A fourth—indirect—feature of surveillance is its context. The technologies now enabling surveillance are the product of very rapid innovation in the early decades of the 21st century, which has significantly altered the character of surveillance. Agreement on what counts as appropriate regulation has been simply unable to keep up thus far. This book, by necessity, reflects these tensions by describing not only what surveillance is like in the 21st century, but also where the fault lines lie and what sorts of efforts are afoot to evaluate and place bounds around surveillance to ensure that it promotes rather than precludes the quest for a fairer and more sustainably human world. There's tension between 'possible' and 'permissible'.

These pressures reflect an ambivalent world of surveillance. Frequently, surveillance is established for a reason with which many would agree, to keep society safe, productive, and governable, to ensure that those who need assistance from the state receive it, to help companies improve their products, to track the course of disease in order to match medical help to need and so on. But the type of agency organizing surveillance, the way data are handled, and the lack—or avoidance—of appropriate regulation may compromise the positive aspirations of those doing surveillance. Such tensions are felt with increasing severity.

All these surveillance features make things—and people associated with them—more visible, whether to the police, employers, government departments, or internet companies. Surveillance is unprecedentedly pervasive as I write. But a parallel shift makes the activities of those doing the surveillance less and less visible to those whose lives are rendered more and more transparent. Visibility is very unevenly distributed. There are many reasons for this, not least that surveillance is embedded in the routines and environments of daily life. Datafied systems have been miniaturized and tucked away like the machinery of an old-fashioned wristwatch so that they are simply not evident or remarkable to the frequent user. Add to which, the benefits of using devices are often perceived by users as outweighing the potential consequences of surveillance.

Surveillance has also become more invisible because of the technically obscure systems by which it operates. Few today claim to understand how a computer system works, any more than they would say they grasp the workings of their car—which today looks more like a computer system than a vehicle. Beyond this, surveillance is achieved by using arcane algorithms, the codes that contain the criteria by which police or marketers find their targets. Such things require complex expertise to understand.

In spite of surveillance itself becoming less visible, people themselves are more and more visible. This social visibility has expanded at an increasing rate in the modern world. In Renaissance Europe few ordinary citizens would have had any idea about the looks let alone the lifestyles of their monarchs. Today, the lives of presidents, prime ministers, and other leaders, and even their families, are often an open book to ordinary citizens. At the same time, we ourselves are also 'seen' more and more by organizations. They may not know us, any more than we could say with confidence that we know the power holders or celebrities whose lives have become more open to us. But what is known *about* us by today's large organizations is both considerable and consequential.

Very few people have a sense of *how* or *why* they are surveilled, not only because of the hidden algorithms but simply because most of these things are not advertised or announced. Security agencies are secretive, and corporations like to guard their procedures. Each entity has its reasons. Furthermore, 'terms of service' agreements, often in small print, lengthy, and in impenetrable jargon, reveal little about surveillance.

Surveillance makes people visible in certain specific ways. You are seen by surveillance not as the complete person known to family, friends, and, of course, yourself, but as someone who watches certain television series, parks a car each day on the same street, enjoys baseball or football, was educated at a particular kind of school, pays taxes in a medium bracket, travels to beaches for vacations, and so forth.

Many consumers have a good idea of what data are collected, and also view this kind of surveillance as a benefit. For instance, the person owning an electric shaver with Bluetooth that tracks a user's motion may be grateful for guidance on 'proper' technique. And, as shaving anything is but a small snippet of someone's day, it may seem trivial to their whole life. However, the case of menstrual apps shows there *are* significant consequences of such for for-profit enterprises, beyond possibly inaccurate period tracking. In the USA, no law protects women from the misuse of their data, for example in workplace pregnancy discrimination.

Clearly, the surveilled are only partially visible to each agency or organization. However, it is also true that these fragments of personal data become connected as data are shared for various reasons—economic, governance—thus creating a more complex picture. This still does not mean that you would recognize the image as yours. Only your data-double is visible to organizations, however complex it becomes.

Multi-directional surveillance

So far, this chapter has commented on the many ways that surveillance occurs, and especially the ways that we as citizens, consumers, and so on become more visible even as our surveillors become less so. The story is complicated, so I also point to some key ways that surveillance operates today and indicate that our everyday lives are increasingly pulled into the surveillance picture, for both better and worse.

Now we ask some questions about the *direction* of surveillance before turning to the range of contexts—from search-and-rescue missions to totalitarian dictatorships—in which surveillance is found. These illustrate how surveillance is a multi-directional way of making others visible and even of making ourselves visible to ourselves and others.

A common, somewhat gloomy view of surveillance pits us against them, where they, as it were, look down on us from on high. And while this understanding of surveillance is frequently accurate, variations do exist. Surveillance by police or the taxation department is necessarily top-down, but there are situations where the gaze may be reversed.

Crowds at a protest march may photograph police activities on their phones, for instance, as they move demonstrators along or arrest them. This is sometimes called *sousveillance*—watching from below. In this example, *sousveillance* is watching-back; the watchers are being watched.

Surveillance can also be not so much top-down as horizontal, between peers, and participatory. This is 'social surveillance'. People watch each other, and their cats, constantly, online. But the twist is this: the platforms not only permit but are designed to facilitate such mutual watching. They make their millions from multiplying and monetizing such everyday connections within surveillance capitalism. Why? Because their intimate user-monitoring makes money, mainly for global internet platforms. They must generate enough content to occupy people spending increasingly more time online. Social surveillance also furnishes data for vertical, top-down surveillance by the same platforms.

Vertical surveillance is especially evident in the activities of national security agencies, of which the United States (US) National Security Agency (NSA) is a prime example. However, as there is extensive collaboration between agencies, especially within the so-called Five Eyes of Australia, Canada, New Zealand, the United Kingdom (UK), and the USA, it is not inappropriate to think of global eyes-in-the-sky. Except that, while satellites or drones are literally in the sky, many crucial components of national security operations are housed in remote and tightly guarded ground-level or underground facilities and intercept communications passing through fibre optic cables that are both subterranean (under continents) and submarine (under oceans).

The NSA and Five Eyes hit the news in 2013 when people were outraged to discover that these agencies sought information not only on those suspected of planning terrorist attacks, but also on ordinary citizens with no previous criminal record. Even presidents and prime ministers were not exempt; President Dilma Roussef of Brazil and Chancellor Angela Merkel of Germany found that their private telephone calls had been monitored.

A spectrum of surveillance

Surveillance takes numerous forms, many of which may be welcomed. Few would deny the value of surveillance programmes aimed at checking on threatened and endangered species or for search-and-rescue (SAR) missions, for instance. Since the early 2010s, drones, outfitted to collect vital data about disaster victims, have become increasingly important for SAR missions, especially after natural disasters. Such events, highly threatening to human life, require rapid responses and accurate relief management, if the human toll is to be minimized. Drones can perform careful reconnaissance missions in areas that are inaccessible or where clear and present danger, such as forest fire or snow avalanche, is present. Elements such as electro-optical sensors, vision cameras, and real-time processing can help detect and locate wounded and missing persons, thus aiding the relief management system.

Such surveillance is in a sense soft, innocuous, and is unlikely to penetrate our privacy or fetter our freedom. It is geared for saving lives and reducing the impact of disaster. Equally, many support the use of surveillance technologies to ensure that industrial companies adhere to environmental standards, that financial organizations are not committing fraud, to protect people from criminal behaviour, or to add another dimension to nursing care for elderly people—especially those suffering from dementia—in residential settings, or even at home. I know family members who are grateful for surveillant wristbands worn by relatives with Alzheimer's who may wander out of the home.

Indeed, in an era when populations are ageing due to declining fertility and rising life expectancy, keeping healthy is more tricky. Cost-effective and easy-to-use remote health monitoring comes into its own, allowing older people to live safely at home, wearing appropriate sensors, sometimes embedded in textile clothing. Heart rate, blood pressure, body temperature, motion, and the like can be checked by sensors. Even tests such as electrocardiograms can be done at a distance. Connections can be made through Bluetooth, along with Personal Digital Assistants and smartphones, all of which are reassuring for both people with health challenges and their families. Of course, these devices will never *substitute* for human contact. And as with all surveillance, data circulating in such systems are vulnerable to misuse and require careful regulation. But their benefits are palpable.

Debates will always arise, however, when persons or populations are monitored, because surveillance is never neutral. Public health surveillance checks, for instance, on the incidence of disease as it is affected by things such as proximity to nuclear power plants or viruses carried on aeroplanes or by migratory birds. Problems may arise, however, in health surveillance systems such as digital 'contact-tracing' apps to slow the spread of infections during the COVID-19 pandemic.

Classic contact-tracing is carried out manually, by public health personnel such as nurses, on the ground. Such surveillance practices have a good track record as an efficient and effective way of determining how the virus is spreading and therefore how to respond with other measures. But digital contact-tracing does not necessarily have such a good reputation. For instance, because the locations of particular groups are traceable within contact-tracing systems, and without humans-in-the-loop, minority groups, women, and even specific businesses may be subject to unwanted or negative treatment that challenges human rights.

At the far end of the spectrum are systems that seem to bristle with threats, to our dignity, freedom, or peace of mind, whose intentions are not only to control our bodies but our thoughts as well. Even systems such as facial recognition, when associated with video cameras to which police have access, or even to online products, exhibit many potential and actual flaws. Many police departments defend their use of facial recognition technologies, but where do they obtain their images? Some are official police photos, but police are also known to use facial recognition for otherwise unknown suspects. Then the images may come from drivers' licences or other records, or may even come from social media.

Worse, surveillance may directly serve the cause of evil and violence, or its prolongation. During the civil war period in Guatemala—1960s to 1996—after the USA had helped depose democratic leaders and replace them with military presidents, mass murder became cruelly commonplace. Many thousands of Mayan people were brutally killed in rural villages, while in cities, journalists, teachers, lawyers, and other professionals were targeted.

They were identified through an elaborate surveillance system, then captured, tortured, and killed by the *Policia nacional*. The neatly classified, typed records of that surveillance (Figure 3) survived—just—providing an appalling account of how ordinary citizens were made to disappear. The police surveillance rendered them visible in order to eliminate them.

In this case, surveillance is clearly a tool of authoritarian rule, something also seen in countries like the German Democratic Republic—think of the film, *The Lives of Others*—or Chile, as we'll see in the next chapter. In such places, surveillance was used as a means of control, where fear of the system was itself a powerful

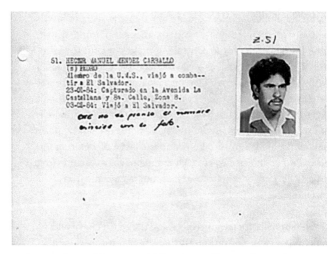

3. A manual surveillance record from 1980s Guatemala.

means of crushing dissent, alongside the actual disappearances, imprisonments, or murders. This is surveillance with a hard, sharp edge, used not only in exceptional circumstances such as war or pandemics, when some normal rules are temporarily suspended, but as a routine technique to cow the population into compliance.

But surveillance does not have to be hard in this extreme sense, to raise questions. Many regard social media and consumer surveillance as 'soft', or relatively harmless. After all, social media offers positive opportunities for 'connecting' with others, especially, for example, during a pandemic. But much social media surveillance involves addictive and manipulatory tactics and, in any case, some apparently soft surveillance can create a slippery slope to much harder kinds.

In what follows, I discuss how surveillance has become so significant in the modern world and especially in today's digital times. Is this just a story of developing technologies that enable such influential but invisible surveillance to occur or is there also something shaping those technologies themselves? We tackle that in the next chapter before turning to the central question of how and with what consequences data has become key to contemporary surveillance. These data, as we have seen, are also involved when we do our own surveillance, joining police quests for crime data, following online clues to find out about others, as we create a culture of surveillance, where watching is a way of life.

Then, we have to ask, in a world suffused with surveillance, how do we decide which surveillance is appropriate—that is, fair and contributing to human flourishing—and which is not? Such ethical issues are of the essence. What are the politics of surveillance? Should we resist, regulate, or relax? How do we discern the likely, the depressing, or the desirable futures of today's surveillance trends?

Chapter 3
Surveillance technologies in context

The smartphone is a universal symbol of connectivity. Carried handily in a pocket, it provides music wherever you are, contact with parents, children, or friends, a means of taking and sharing amazing videos and photos, news and weather reports on the go, quick texts—'I'm running late'—the ability to check email or internet, or to pay the bus fare, to work remotely; the list is long. It pervades all of society; remember Barack Obama, the first smartphone President, with his faithful Canadian Blackberry? Or when your 8-year-old pleaded for her own?

However, the smartphone *should* also be seen as a universal symbol of surveillance. While nothing need be retracted from the previous paragraph, the smartphone is also a primary conduit for surveillance in the 21st century. Millions of people carry these personal tracking devices with them every day and every use sends signals to multiple data-users, to be shared, sold, reused in both mundane and extraordinary ways.

This chapter looks at surveillance technologies from several different angles. It starts with what at the end of the last century was—and to some still is—the key symbol of surveillance, the CCTV camera, seen as a mode of remote policing. This displays the ambivalence of surveillance and also the ways that its technological development is not an autonomous process. People often think of new kinds of society being *produced* by technology, but it is equally important to note that new technologies are also *the product* of specific social, economic, and political arrangements.

Surveillance today is the product of many different impulses, and is held together in mutable, shifting forms that we can think of as 'assemblages'. We explore how this happens and also show how much surveillance is far less direct than before. However, returning to the technology–society interaction, the chapter ends by considering how surveillance helps to shape our social relationships.

The ambivalent eye

Today, before writing this, a sign on the wall of the doctor's office told me why there's a little camera in a corner. Residents, physicians in their final two years of training, are sometimes observed while they discuss the patient's current ailment. This way, the supervising doctor can advise and support them on their performance as aspiring family physicians. The sign not only explains the purpose behind the camera, but also allows patients to opt out if they wish. Sitting there, I was glad for the explanation, but also for the care taken in preparing doctors for their independent practice. Benign surveillance on a local scale, I concluded.

In the 1990s, Closed Circuit Television (CCTV) expanded enormously in the streets of the UK. The trigger was the capture on film of the child murderers of James Bulger in 1993. The footage from this horrific scene showed the boys leading the toddler away from his mother; police say it played a vital role in catching the killers. The evidence was widely accepted as clear proof of the utility of CCTV for solving crimes, if not, by optimistic extension, preventing them. Britain put hundreds of millions of pounds into CCTV, making it the central crime control strategy of that country by the mid-1990s.

By the early 2020s, London had given up its position to Taiyuan, China, as the world-leading CCTV city, in terms of cameras per 1,000 people. By that point London was in fourth place, after Chennai and Hyderabad, India, and Harbin, China, if measured by the density of cameras per square kilometre. (China claims that cameras reduce crime, but Taiyuan's crime rates remain relatively high on this scale.) As crime reduction is the primary reason for installing cameras, it is worth finding out how far such systems make a difference.

Several multi-country surveys of criminological research have been produced during the 21st century, and their main conclusions are clear. Overall, the statistically significant evidence shows that CCTV has reduced some crime, although this may be short-lived. In a range of settings, CCTV reduced crime on average by 13 per cent, compared with sites with no CCTV. What kinds of crime? Most noteworthy is a 20 per cent reduction in drug-related crime, followed by a 14 per cent decrease in vehicle and property crime. However, no statistically significant decreases were found for violent crime or public disorder. Moreover, a few studies demonstrate that crime shifts to other places as a result of CCTV presence.

Cameras are not a cure-all for crime. All sorts of factors are significant, from the quality of the footage—often grainy—or the context in which the cameras are placed. The best images are face-on, so a camera pointing down a row of cars in a parking lot may produce usable shots. Other factors include the location or the power of the cameras and the concentration and response speed of camera operators. Despite massive expenditure on CCTV in countries such as South Africa, Colombia, or India, clear evidence of significantly reduced crime rates is thin.

In addition cameras need to be actually working and switched on at the time of the incident, and agreement has to be reached that the footage is admissible in a court of law. Reliable research shows that CCTV is generally unlikely to deter crime, and although this is debated, it is very hard to prove one way or the other. British expert Clive Norris stresses the 'myth of the rational offender' in this context: most offenders do not act on the basis of careful calculation, especially in violent crime.

Despite the research and the well-publicized limitations of cameras to address crime rates, they continue to be installed. And wall- or pole-mounted cameras still offer a clichéd concept of surveillance. Simultaneously, evidence is mounting to challenge the claims that cameras are effective in detecting crime and gathering evidence, reducing the fear of crime, of being a 'perfect witness', or deterring crime. However, installing cameras may give the public the impression that the government is doing something, and they may make people who already feel safe, feel safer, while making no difference to those who already feel unsafe.

There is more to technology than meets the eye. The surveillance 'vision' is always limited. Faith in technology's capacity to ameliorate social problems through surveillance is a theme that affects areas other than CCTV. Bentham was highly optimistic about his panoptic architecture. A wholesale turn to biometrics, data-gathering on ordinary citizens, and militarizing of airports followed 9/11. A similar, and in some ways successful, reflex to deploy 'big data' spiralled with the COVID-19 pandemic in 2020. Trust in technologies arises from the fact that they are developed to ameliorate human problems and that we rely on technology in our daily lives.

But technology does not produce or reproduce itself. For instance, people sometimes say that laws cannot keep pace with technology. There's a sense in which this is self-evident. If smartphones, with their complex multi-functionality, are regulated as if they were conventional landline telephones, on which one can only speak to someone else remotely, most of their functionality will be ignored. But the 'pace' of technological development depends on everything from competition between companies to popular take-up rates. Even 'autonomous' technologies do not make or propel themselves.

In fact, technologies, including ones used for surveillance, are the products of many social, political, economic, and cultural factors. In the classic case of cameras, the *kind* of surveillance that occurs depends on multiple players in the drama. Much more happens than an organizational decision to install cameras, followed by the collection and scrutiny of relevant footage. The technology has to be seen as something *produced* for certain purposes rather than only as *prompting* social and cultural changes.

On the 'supply' side, police, municipalities, media, corporate interests, insurance companies, and a whole amalgam of manufacturers, private security agencies, and consultants press for public space cameras. Some members of the public also demand more cameras, believing that the electronic eye makes them safer. Others, feeling that they may be inappropriately exposed in gendered or racialized ways, shun cameras on principle. The process is messy and mutable at each stage; the actual surveillance is the product of inextricably mixed social and technical factors.

Beyond this, how the technologies relate to their contexts plays a role in improving—or undermining—social relationships. Some, such as biometrics, which uses data obtained from the human body, may face both ways.

Refugee and humanitarian aid programmes, run by the United Nations and other agencies, today include biometric registration. In Nigeria, this is used, for instance, to protect people displaced by Boko Haram, an Islamist militant organization. Humanitarian agencies say that if refugees are registered, they will be better able to ensure that their camps are safe and not suffer from insurgent reprisals. But in another context, researchers have shown that Afghan refugees seeking repatriation experience higher levels of intrusion and insecurity following biometric registration. Different kinds of surveillance technologies present different challenges, and sometimes different threats, in different contexts. They can also constrain or channel surveillance of particular kinds.

Some technologies have effects *not* intended by their creators. Their very existence may mean that they play a role in surveillance processes. If, for instance, the capability exists to collect more data—say from 'open sources' such as social media—those managing such systems might feel compelled to use them, especially if they have been convinced that simply having more data is always beneficial. 'Collect it all' is, among other things, a post-9/11 security agency slogan that expresses just this sentiment.

Yet other technologies seem to appear before they have actually been developed. For example, the 2002 film *Minority Report*, with its 'Pre-Crime' policing department, seemed to presage predictive policing, before it was a serious option in police departments. In the film, information emanates from three psychic 'precogs' and this enables police officers to anticipate crime and apprehend criminals before they act. Predictive policing appears to echo this, using surveillance data for foreknowledge, in order to pre-empt crime. The director of the film, Steven Spielberg, painstakingly interviewed scientists, in order to create credible scenarios for high-tech policing.

New technologies are not stand-alone phenomena that are invented, appear in public, and then have 'impacts'. Technology is better thought of as human activity—doing technology—and thus it never stands alone. Technologies are adopted as a means of achieving some goal, such as improving national security or reducing traffic accidents. As such, all technologies have a historical context. A surveillance technology such as a police drone has a prehistory in the military, dating back to using cameras for reconnaissance in early aeroplanes, but can be now sometimes equipped for gathering data from public wi-fi as well as images of suspicious activity—including thermal images, used for discovering illegal cannabis production, for instance—on the ground.

'Socio-technical' is a good word to describe this world, where technology and social aspects twist and turn in an inescapable dance with each other. Creating and using a police drone is in part an economic response to high policing costs, at a time when drones are becoming culturally acceptable through the proliferation of hobby and delivery drones. But responses to the use of police drones, for instance at political protests, may include complaints of needless military-style intervention. An important tension lies here, between surveillance technology seen in promotional advertising or movies and surveillance technologies actually experienced or used in everyday life.

So, how does this work out in practice? What holds surveillance activities together and how does this affect everyday lives? Which begs further questions, such as what this means in different parts of the world—everyday lives are different depending on where we are. And what means are available for evaluating such surveillance?

Technologies and the surveillance assemblage

Many surveillance technologies are described in this book, but they depend on a variety of data types. These include photographic and video images, such as from CCTV; biometric data, drawing on information from the body, from fingerprints through iris scans to facial geometry; genetic data, from blood, body fluids, hair, or tissue; location data, especially from Global Positioning Satellites

(GPS) and phones; tracking technologies, often relying on Radio Frequency Identification (RFID) and thus triggered by a sensor. However, what they have in common is that these data may be captured, stored, analysed, processed, and shared digitally. This is what makes them both useful and vulnerable.

Each of the technologies just mentioned is *intended* to work surveillantly. Western tech giants did not see themselves as setting up surveillance systems. But their systems are highly surveillant in that they collect and analyse data relating to human subjects that are used, among other things, to improve and to market their products. In so doing they preside over some of the strongest surveillance systems in the world, using sophisticated analytic tools to track, classify, and modify the behaviour of their users and consumers. And something like facial recognition technology—which would readily be seen as surveillant if used by a police department—is an extremely powerful system.

Data first amassed by one of these companies may end up, through transactions with data brokers and other players, including governments, being used by agencies that do engage explicitly in surveillance.

The digital connections between different kinds of data make it possible to move between them for comparison and contrast or to privilege one over another for specific purposes. Global and local digital networks expand constantly, in principle contributing to greater efficiency and also to a rising need for system security. So today's societies depend heavily on surveillance both economically and politically, but also in everyday life.

Whether for medical conditions or driving conditions, surveillance data is deemed essential. Such dependence makes for a very uncertain, fluid, world in which flows and fluctuations of data are, paradoxically, constant. Examples from the surveillance technology industry illustrate this clearly.

The 20th-century marriage of computing and communications, which were previously distinct technological fields, enabled surveillance as we now know it. What that merger accelerated was the exponentially increased flow of data both within organizations and, crucially, between them. And because the eventual networks based on these flows were also international, this meant that data could be shared in novel ways, facilitating new modes of cooperation between both companies and nation-states. As everyone has become more dependent on digital infrastructures in daily life—phones, computers, homes, appliances, vehicles, streets, and stores are increasingly connected—so surveillance becomes routine and taken for granted.

A word commonly used to describe this situation of diverse things and processes brought together in interconnected networks is *assemblage*. This is a cluster of things, activities, processes, and people that are found working together or at least *aligned*. An example of a surveillant assemblage is the clustering of systems dependent on widely available technologies for mass, rather than targeted, surveillance.

Police in many countries, for example, often use data from social media as they try to track and prevent crime. The assemblage is created on the basis of a desire to connect, believing that to do so would be beneficial, for control, management, security, entertainment, and probably for profit as well. Philosopher Gilles Deleuze likened the assemblage to a ground-creeper, technically a 'rhizome', a plant that grows horizontally and seemingly haphazardly.

The assemblage ingests many kinds of data emanating from bodies—images from CCTV, sensor data from the supermarket, clicks on internet pages, biometric data, and so on—transforming them into usable information for an endless variety of purposes.

The assemblage creates 'data-doubles', or data-selves. These become the source of information about those whose activities were captured in the first place and may affect their lives in both trivial and life-changing ways. Surveillance today rarely has a 'person' in view. Rather, surveillance systems disassemble and reassemble personal data into informational flows that are stabilized and captured by pre-established classificatory criteria. They are then reassembled, using algorithms, in ways that suit institutional demands, and can often also be linked back to the person who provided the data in the first place.

The data-double is always mutating. It is intrinsically unstable and, in that sense, unreliable without other information, preferably supplied by the individual concerned, but also through data. But this raises complex questions to which we can only hint at responses here. Our lives are now shaped, in part, by our relationships with data and this affects many things, such as how we are 'seen', represented, and treated.

As 'personal' data originate and circulate in and between both commercial and administrative settings, as well as traditionally personal ones, special care is called for. Amazon or Netflix might not worry if they make a few data errors in predicting books or movies you would like, but in other contexts—such as the military, national security, banking, policing, health, or welfare—such mistakes might mean life or death. And, importantly, they are *felt* differently, depending on the context. Interconnected databases and advanced analytics may have both relatively trivial and potentially tragic surveillance effects.

Surveillance technologies in context

The earlier example of camera surveillance, though instructive, is discussed above in relation primarily to the UK and the USA. The same features may not hold elsewhere. In Mexico, for example, and indeed in Central and South America, things are often seen differently. For one thing, neither violence against children nor concerns about terrorism is the key issue. Frequently, the hot button issue for many involved in crime control in Central and Latin America is public security in which armed violence flares up especially, but not only, in urban settings. This includes, prominently, gang violence, sometimes associated with drug trafficking, which involves guns.

Surveillance technologies such as CCTV or biometric identification have been widely used in this context, as a means of combating such violence, and improving public security. Until recently, however, such technologies were frequently viewed in some Latin American countries as a purely technical matter, not requiring investigation in their own right. But to miss seeing surveillance technologies as an aspect of social organization relating to crime control is to miss the very meaning of those technologies. They do not exist on their own. They are the products of specific conditions that give life to them. And this is as true in Myanmar or Madagascar as it is in Mexico.

The historical-cultural contexts are often forgotten, especially in an era when the digital seem to rule supreme. A memory gap exists between Max Weber's exposé of 19th- and early 20th-century 'rational' administrative record-keeping, where everything was measured and calculated, creating an increasingly impersonal 'iron cage', and the computer-based techniques of the later 20th century. Yet, this 'gap' was an important period for inventing quickly popular 'evidence-based' surveillance technologies, notably the portable camera, the telephone, and the phonograph. Each made previously less visible activities more visible and complicated relationships between being private or public.

The late 19th-century forensic focus on items such as handwriting, fingerprints, and unconscious thought was matched by the development of the camera, for the recorded image, phonography for the recorded voice, and the telephone for remote eavesdropping. In terms of felt threats, these new media added to the perceived risks of losing control over one's persona, and thus reputation. They could even be reproduced for more public consumption. For example, cameras were used to embarrass drinkers in dry American states. Inventor Thomas Edison thought that his phonograph could eliminate the need for stenographers or typists, including making a 'perfect record' that could be secretly transmitted. Entertainment was not on his mind. And the telephone enabled the now legendary listening-in by switchboard operators (Figure 4).

4. Telephone operators, London, 1950s.

Historian Josh Lauer notes that it's not the simple existence of these new technologies that made them surveillant. Certainly, one's image, words, and deeds could exist beyond one's control. But it is the proliferation of evidence in some 'new medium'—the photograph, for instance—produced, stored, and publicized by institutions and individuals, that makes the difference to questions of privacy or power. These new media enabled surveillance, but they only *became* surveillant when used for that purpose. The same cannot be said, of course, for technologies such as CCTV that are made to be surveillant or have intrinsically surveillant capacities. Context, again, is crucial.

The other critical context is political economy, which is about how production and trade intersect with law and government. Again, the historical record shows with stark clarity how some of the most severe and sinister forms of surveillance are associated with extreme kinds of political economy. These range from early 1930s Nazi use of commercially available punch card technology to identify German Jews from the census, mid-20th-century Soviet communism issuing passports in order to crackdown on dissidents in Poland or Ukraine, to military dictatorship in Chile following the US-backed coup that displaced Salvador Allende in 1973. The threat has not evaporated today.

The KGB in the Soviet Union amassed vast amounts of information through interrogation, telephone tapping, and many other means. Until the 1980s they were developing techniques such as voice recognition for intercepting phone calls. In Chile, the military junta under Pinochet maintained a high level of surveillance activities, some of which may be seen today in a Santiago museum. In its basement are the twisted wires of the communications centre that listened in on civilian conversations. Note that this surveillance was still *targeted*, not yet the 'mass' surveillance of the post-9/11 era. Each of these exemplified totalitarian goals that can be achieved only by a brutal crackdown on dissent, using surveillance as the tool.

These examples might make those in liberal democracies feel a sense of relief or reassurance, as they enjoy legally enshrined checks and balances against such extremes and excesses of state surveillance. However, while there are indeed laws and traditions that exist to reduce the risk of totalitarian despotism in many countries, these do not guarantee that such conditions—or their effects—could not be reproduced in an era of surveillance capitalism. The gargantuan global growth of state surveillance after 9/11, frequently and ironically dependent on consumer monitoring and tracking—recall the surveillant assemblage—has produced a situation in which, once again, the underlying political economy engenders technological developments that support regimes reminiscent of the totalitarian. In the 21st century, several countries lean heavily towards authoritarian populism, enabled partly by these new technologies.

Even security agencies in 'liberal democracies' engage in 'suspicionless' or 'mass' surveillance. The monitoring of legitimate political dissent, such as opposing oil pipeline development, is very disturbing for protesters. Political parties may depend on some arguably undemocratic means of maintaining power, such as micro-targeting profiled voters with customized messages in the USA and elsewhere. So the need for public vigilance has certainly not waned. In this large-scale context of political economy, which may be considered as a 'surveillance-industrial-complex', surveillance technologies proliferate in sophisticated and subtle ways.

In countries of the global south, fragile democracies struggle with similar issues. While state surveillance is not unimportant, political-economic pressures from large corporations are often harbingers of increasing surveillance. Some, like Meta, partner with mobile carriers for such countries to have 'free' internet services. This may benefit those otherwise unable to get online but it also provides new markets for them and can also expose them to unfamiliar modes of surveillance.

Surveillance technologies mediate social relationships

Today, while some direct surveillance—using eyes and ears—still exists, the overwhelming majority of surveillance practices are ways of seeing that do not depend on eyesight: they are 'mediated' versions of visibility. New equipment from TV to smartphones facilitates such mediated visibility, says communications sociologist John Thompson, now increasingly available to all. The surveillance activities of multinational technology conglomerates mediate user visibility, but they in turn may also be the means by which its users become aware of what such companies do.

A key aspect of life in the modern world is the way that direct social relationships have increasingly given way to indirect ones, a central theme of sociology (see Georg Simmel's ideas on the stranger, an expanding category in modernizing European cities, above). Our relations with strangers are only indirect. But what lies behind this shift, which increases the proportion of indirect relationships? Changes in transportation and communication technologies are crucial, so that increasingly people are in touch with others who are physically absent.

Social media plays a huge role here today (not least, and to the benefit of many, in the time of modern pandemics). We sacrifice co-presence for the immediacy and reach of mediated interaction. Much social life today is more about contact—though not necessarily actual encounters—with strangers rather than with families and neighbours. During the later 20th century, the growth of information technology helped to speed the expansion of indirect relationships.

Social analyst Craig Calhoun suggests that in addition to what were once thought of as primary and secondary relations, in which people are present to each other, are tertiary relations with no co-presence, mediated by machines or other people. The relationship between voters and their representatives in national politics is an example, but the people involved are still aware of these relationships and some mutual recognition is important.

Beyond this is the ballooning category of 'quaterniary' relationships, dependent especially on the internet, that have no necessary knowledge of who the others are in those relationships. When someone in India or Korea, unknown to me, wants to connect with me on an internet site, they are using a quaterniary relationship to try to establish a tertiary or even a secondary relationship.

Surveillance produces such relationships by monitoring actions and communicating them, regardless of what the surveilled subjects intend or want. Such surveillance could be any kind of tracing of communications and data, through smartphones, credit cards, filing taxes online, watching television, driving a car, claiming medical benefits, using a pedometer, buying a ticket for a bus, plane, or train or entering a building. Those data are analysed by unknown others, primarily machines, and circulate in ways that alert yet other individuals or systems. They are indirect, unseen, and yet powerful relationships.

However, the example of social media highlights another aspect of this. While surveillance makes ordinary life visible to those in authority or power, whether economic or political, those powers themselves have in weaker ways also become more visible to ordinary citizens through new media. The few may watch the many, as Foucault observed in the Panopticon, but the many also have more and more opportunities to watch the few. Sociologist Thomas Mathiesen called this the 'synopticon'. This occurred especially through television in the last century but now, even more, through the internet. And on the internet the many also watch the many.

The internet is implicated in surveillance in many other ways, too. The next section reminds us that surveillance is big business, in both domestic and international contexts. The 'surveillance assemblage' shows up again here.

Selling surveillance technologies

In an era of remote shopping, doorstep piracy, where packages delivered are often stolen, new 'solutions' spring to life. One such solution is video doorbells, and very soon after their introduction police departments were obtaining customer permission to use their footage. Within a couple of years, this turned into the largest corporate-owned citizen-installed surveillance system in the USA. Millions of householders also use crime-reporting apps, to which content can be uploaded from video doorbells. Law enforcement can obtain footage without a warrant and tens of thousands of such requests were made in 2020–1 alone.

This convergence of technologies and social practices is another good example of the surveillance assemblage. But in practice, if householders' alerts are weighted heavily along racial lines, and these are also available to cooperating police departments, the technology could be used in some socially unequal and unaccountable ways.

While social media companies and consumer marketing agencies may not sell their wares as 'surveillance' technologies, this example shows that many other companies deliberately do so. Many household brand computer technology and internet companies assist national security and policing agencies in ways that are not only less than visible but sometimes less than responsible. Such corporations state that all they do is to produce the technologies, while the onus for how they are used lies with the customer.

Moving away from household consumer markets, however, we find many companies that sell surveillance technologies worldwide. The world's largest exporters are the USA, UK, France,

Germany, and Israel. According to Privacy International, of the 528 surveillance companies that they list, 87 per cent are in OECD countries, 75 per cent are in NATO member states. They include the following: Internet Service Providers (ISPs) that often have to ensure that their networks are accessible to government agencies; telecommunications equipment vendors sell hardware that is often designed for ease of surveillance use; surveillance companies sell technologies such as hidden bugs, Global Positioning System (GPS) tracking systems, or miniature cameras for law enforcement and intelligence gathering.

While some exported surveillance devices are of this classic type, others for sale are simply secret, such as equipment for monitoring internet communications on a mass scale, malware that can, for example, switch on your computer's camera, or smartphone monitoring systems that can activate phones to connect with them, for example, to identify protesters at a demonstration.

Appraising surveillance technologies

Surveillance today is overwhelmingly technology assisted. Technology does not determine or direct surveillance, but contemporary surveillance is facilitated by new technologies. Also, the technologies themselves play a role within the sociotechnical systems of today's surveillance, constraining and enabling what is possible. Surveillance often employs technologies to enhance the visibility of subjects and today this is central. Simultaneously, emerging technological infrastructures permit surveillance to occur without their being directly observed.

But technological potential is not social destiny. Whatever is claimed for the system will invariably be modified in practice; the system may fail or not work as advertised, users may subvert or interfere with the system, deliberately or inadvertently. For example, efforts to make camera systems 'smart' depend on very sophisticated technologies for noting movements, recognizing faces, and tracking persons. But this requires massive investment in converting CCTV images into MPEG4s and then applying high-level analytics.

Evidence that these practices might 'work' is elusive. Equally, those who know they are 'on CCTV' may not merely 'smile' but play up to or, equally, evade or ignore the cameras. In other areas, air passengers who are members of visible minority groups may organize their passage through airport security for minimum delay.

Surveillance is seldom stand-alone. Usually, it involves many technologies working together in a loose, liquid, and mutating assemblage. The technologies never operate by themselves, however. They are driven by the felt need for greater reliability or convenience, faith in their capabilities, the urge to collect more and more data, and the quest for efficiency and for profit. Corporate competition is strong, whether for law enforcement and anti-terrorism or between internet platforms.

Personal data is at a premium within these systems, valued for both its crime-control and commercial aspects. But this data goes far beyond obvious facts such as name, address, and date of birth. Because of this, critical decisions must be made about encryption, data protection, cyber-security, and above all the appropriate uses of personal data. But also about how to inform the *generators* of such data—ordinary people in daily life—of how profoundly significant for their life chances these seemingly trivial bits of data are. GPS coordinates and purchasing patterns may seem mundane but their consequences can be momentous.

So what should be the typical image of surveillance? Pole-mounted cameras or the smartphone? As we have seen, other kinds of data than visual images, such as from smartphones, are far more significant for surveillance today, even though the visual is still highly important. All these technologies serve to make individuals and groups more visible to organizations. And even if that visibility is metaphorical it is often very consequential, for both good and ill. The technologies are also ambiguous in their effects and their effectiveness and thus need to be understood in their specific contexts and evaluated in ways that go beyond simplistic calls for efficiency, productivity, and cost-effectiveness.

Chapter 4
Data-driven surveillance: new challenges

Platforms were once thought of as an elevated area in a station for boarding trains, raised flooring to enable musicians or politicians to be seen by an audience, or perhaps a structure from which wild birds might be watched. Today, 'platform' also designates a particular kind of business, a company using an application or website from which its service is offered. More exactly, says author Nick Srnicek, they are businesses—from Google through Microsoft to Airbnb—that provide the hardware and software foundation for others to operate on. Such platforms have mushroomed rapidly to become a prominent feature of 21st-century society.

Platforms depend on data, gathered from multiple sources, and such data-gathering is inescapably surveillant, relying as it does on everyday involvement of people going about their daily lives in digital environments. But this does not exhaust the definition. Several such platforms show a marked tendency to be monopolistic and even to view themselves as going beyond mere economic entities to undertaking some government-like tasks. These household-name giant corporations now dominate stock markets as they trade in gathering, dissecting, and reassembling massive amounts of everyday data, which in turn starts to shape the lives and communities of those who unwittingly provided the data in the first place.

Of course, platforms also depend on their popularity with millions of people around the world. They produce generally easy-to-use interfaces to online sites that offer quick and satisfactory solutions to needs for all manner of services, from keeping in touch with family and friends to ordering a ride or finding an overnight stay. And when circumstances change, platforms nimbly appear to fill the niche. Food delivery services arrived almost overnight as a godsend when COVID-19 struck, drastically reducing possibilities for eating out. The data they gather tells them a lot about food preferences—and much else—in different postcodes and segments of the population.

Such popularity should not be underestimated. Although consumers may move from one platform to another when they become dissatisfied, the steady rise in smartphone use indicates clearly that the appetite for usable and trustworthy platforms seems undiminished. Education, journalism, conventional TV and radio, as well as commerce all have altered their content and style to accommodate the platform world, surveillance and all.

One way to think of this new development within capitalism is to refer to 'data-driven surveillance'. This does not mean that the process is autonomous, of course. Those data are deliberately gathered so that they can be analysed, using algorithms, for the various purposes that platform companies have in mind. It is difficult to overstate the significance of this very hypermodern development which, as we shall see in a moment, is a close cousin of 'surveillance capitalism'. But it hasn't escaped the attention of a popular TV series.

The satirical series, *Black Mirror*, in an episode called 'Nosedive', depicts a young woman, Lacie, who lives in an America where all interactions are rated on an app that syncs with a device allowing users to see the rankings in real time. A disturbing dimension of 'Nosedive' is its portrayal of technology, not in some sci-fi future, but reflecting aspects of real life in the 21st century.

Today, quantification and ranking is everywhere, including, especially, on social media. The system depends on accumulating 'likes' just as, in the fictional world of 'Nosedive', one's reputation is built up or blasted by one's peers. This is a continuous process, without let-up, in which the stakes can rise or fall overnight, or faster. Lacie works hard to boost her scores, preening herself in front of the mirror or highly rating those who serve her coffee in hope of a similar return rating. But when her luck runs out, the world turns savagely against her, refusing her access to services, shunning her in public, and generally making her feel a failure and a misfit.

Most discussions of the 'Nosedive' episode see the unsettling resemblance to social media and the ways in which everyday life is vulnerable to the amplified judgements of others. Self-curation and affirmation-seeking are commonplace features of the social media saturated world, so these consequences are unsurprising. One's social standing, acceptability for employment, and access to services increasingly depend in part on that precious peer-produced persona. The platforms that collect data originating in likes, followers, and preferences of all kinds expressed online sell those data to other corporations such that the information circulates among marketers. Police and government organizations often have access, too, using those same data for different purposes. What is valued by marketers is also sought-after raw material for all manner of judgements.

While the 'Nosedive' satire accurately lampoons a social media-addicted world, there is another reality behind the everyday quantification. Many modern societies are indeed dependent on rating and ranking everyone, which in turn relies on massive data surveillance, but this is not merely or even mainly peer produced. The whole edifice of contemporary marketing depends on evaluating consumers, with a view to determining their 'lifetime value'. What you are worth to the corporation determines how the corporation treats you. The scoring is based on many activities—

shopping, drinking coffee, ordering pizza or cars, along with staying at a property—that people engage in on a regular basis.

This is the basic drive of surveillance capitalism, drawing our attention to the success of internet corporations. Everyday involvement with phones, tablets, laptops, and other devices such as fitness apps or digital assistants is a conduit, not just for personal data as occasional or discrete bits of information, but for a flood of details about who you are, where you are going, what music or movies you prefer, who your friends are, and so on. Internet companies obtain the data at minimal cost and sell the bulk data to other companies as well as using the data for their own purposes.

Based on an analysis of these business models, Shoshana Zuboff shows how internet companies obtain access to the real-time flow of daily life in the hope of influencing a person's behaviour for profit. The companies believe that getting their hands on the data will enable them subtly to alter people's outlooks and activities such that they become more and more dependent on the goods and services that they produce and market. Flags raised by this go far beyond privacy. They include a potential for undermining self-determination and even democracy. For Zuboff, it smacks of what illiberal and authoritarian *states* sometimes try to achieve and thus challenges the basic tenets of Western liberal democracy.

As surveillance capitalism spreads, warn the critics, it erodes the limits and legal regulations by government that were once placed on commercial practices. Those limits and regulations included binding contracts and understandings between corporations, employees, and consumers. The problem is that social participation—think employment, education, healthcare—now largely depends upon internet access and the use of tools privately owned by corporations.

The surveillance capitalist future is, in a sense, a worst-case scenario, albeit one that many companies might like to emulate. Any who aspire to be a major player may also want to use profuse data to increase operational efficiency as well as to gain insights into consumer behaviour and preferences. However, many companies that would like to get on the big data bandwagon have a hard time doing so, just because they started out long before those data-as-key-resource corporations appeared. Their already-existing systems are not easy to upgrade.

After all, not only in the global north but increasingly in the global south, whole populations rely on the benefits of the online world for their daily interactions with all kinds of service providers. If the logic of capitalist accumulation really does come to be based on the involuntary and invisible extraction of data from ordinary users by these private corporations, the tensions between participation and exploitation could create new social cleavages and conflicts.

What happens when surveillance becomes 'data-driven?' We first follow the story of how this occurred, and spell out some of its implications. It becomes clear why 'data-driven' is in quotation marks. A discussion of four kinds of application, in policing, national security, humanitarian aid, and political elections, follows, and the chapter wraps up with some important questions common to big data surveillance.

How data became central

Until the early 21st century, the internet was used mainly as a *source* of information; you could find things out, easily and quickly, from news and weather or the stock market and from 'how things work' to historical facts and genealogy. But web 2.0, dependent on user-generated content, quickly caught on from the turn of the century, which prompted a fresh focus on data.

Not that data just 'appeared' at that time—databases had been in existence for decades—but their potential for profit-making and new modes of analysis was realized and with it a new expression: 'big data'. Google was among the first to work out how to monetize what was at first described as 'data exhaust', while numerous other bodies from healthcare to national security agencies became interested in the possibilities of extracting value from the vast volume of data now deluging the internet.

The various practices associated with the blanket term 'big data' have many surveillance outcomes beyond social media platforms, in predictive policing, consumer analytics, data-driven national security, and big data healthcare among others. Unfortunately, data analytics of various sorts is often seen as the saviour, even though big data itself is seldom satisfactorily defined. Other descriptors are added, such as 'volume, variety, and velocity' of data, to which others such as veracity may be added. And of course, the huge amount of data, obtained from diverse sources and analysed at high speed *does* give clues about what constitutes 'big data'.

These Vs do not *define* big data, however. For critics danah boyd and Kate Crawford, avoiding the big data buzzword means focusing on the 'capacity for researchers to search, aggregate and cross-reference large data-sets'. This clear definition of big data underlies what is written here. It indicates a capacity for very large-scale collecting and analysing data, for many possible purposes. Some such purposes have obvious potential human benefit, from understanding climate change to improving public health to relieving urban traffic congestion.

However, care is still needed because big data interventions are often accompanied by a mythology—communications specialist José van Dijck aptly calls this 'dataism'—which suggests that big data represents a 'scientific revolution' in which efforts aimed at, for instance, finding explanations—theories about *causes*, in other words—should give way to seeking *correlations* between data phenomena as adequate ways of understanding.

At the same time, in the realm of data*ism*, data is often viewed as neutral or disinterested. To indulge in dataism is to suppose that just having access to data and the means to analyse it offers big advantages. But data are never raw. The word data comes from the Latin, 'things that are given', but they do not in fact exist as data until someone decides to consider them as such and to collect and analyse them according to certain criteria. Data are further 'cooked' using algorithms.

Put simply, algorithms are codes that solve problems by following a series of instructions. For example, imagine you are making dinner; you follow a recipe for the best results. You have either tested the recipe, modifying it for improvements, or you rely on someone else's testing. Algorithms are analogous to recipes in this sense. Now, the algorithms used in laboratory science are one thing. Such environments are very controlled and the data areas as clean as possible. This is far from true in areas such as policing. It makes all the difference who creates the algorithms and decides on their use as these codes filter for particular criteria. Especially in the world of surveillance.

Situating data surveillance

In 1988, Australian computer scientist Roger Clarke introduced the concept of 'dataveillance' to describe how, increasingly, populations are 'seen'—made visible—using data rather than through direct means such as physical hearing or seeing. Little did he know how much this would expand in the following decades. Visibility was rapidly enhanced at an industrial scale especially as surveillance operations of all kinds became more automated and data dependent.

If indiscriminate gathering of data is one feature of so-called big data surveillance, then the move beyond targeted and systematic data collection and analysis is another. This is generalized surveillance, often called 'mass' surveillance, but perhaps better thought of—in a national security context—as 'suspicionless' surveillance, at the point of collection. 'Mass' surveillance becomes a reality as soon as the data are analysed. If surveillance beyond borders was already a signature of surveillance at a global level, then this portends surveillance without limits.

A final feature of this is that the data are mined and analysed using algorithms. Again, it has always been necessary to work out how to focus a surveillance operation, but in earlier times the trail of coding could be traced back to the police, marketing, or intelligence strategy that initiated it. Now algorithms are used that themselves may be enhanced by AI and Machine Learning methods. So not only are the data of possibly dubious quality in the first place, how they are handled is partly within an automated system that may allow for little human discretion.

The algorithms are needed because without them, analysing the mountains of data for patterns and correlations would be impossible. But as analysts sometimes acknowledge, even they do not necessarily know exactly why the algorithms 'work'. They are essential if partially inexplicable tools. And they are invisible, seen only from their inputs and outputs. In everyday life, people are aware of them when, for instance, a website autoplays other videos matching your tastes beyond the one on which you clicked. Algorithms and machine-learning are embedded with human-created purposes, they are not created in a vacuum.

National security agencies operate using algorithms. They collect huge amounts of data, requiring algorithm-coding for interpretation. Terrorism, though terrible, is a relatively rare event. Set the algorithms, the rules for interpreting, too tight and terrorists may strike with no warning. But set them too loosely and many other innocents may get caught in the dragnet. In these scenarios, it could be that algorithms should be thanked for averting attacks or blamed for persons wrongfully on no-fly lists or, worse, subject to extraordinary rendition and torture.

With data surveillance, the data-image or data-self becomes a crucial determinant of life chances and choices. The actual activities of the human body become less critical as video surveillance and computer monitoring—plus today, the internet and social media, including voice-activated assistants—scrutinize everyday actions, permitting and denying access or eligibility as a result. These technologies of control open and close doors in everyday life. Reduced to a data-image, Deleuze comments that it is no longer an 'individual' that is seen by surveillance but a 'dividual.' The dividual's card, code or bodily trace is all that counts for the system, not the embodied person.

Despite dividual status, data, however fragmented and volatile, both arise from and make a difference to real ordinary lives. Data are extracted, routinely, from those everyday lives, in a world where the once-trusted notion of consent has largely been evacuated of meaning. We might question how people can consent meaningfully to a process they do not realize is occurring and whose inner workings are mysterious to the non-expert.

The critical factor is the data record. The way data may be used for or against us marks us as dividuals. Such dividuals can be divided and subdivided endlessly. The data may be taken from the human body but is soon recombined beyond human control, based on institutional criteria, now translated into algorithms. Individual humans have agency, but where are they left if actual decisions about life chances and choices depend on control mechanisms that reduce persons to dividuals?

Data also become implicated in social sorting and social ordering in new ways. Inequalities may be ameliorated, but also deepened, using new data-analysing methods. The following examples from predictive policing, national security, and humanitarian aid illustrate this.

Predictive policing

Predictive policing is about how data may be used to say what sorts of criminal activity are likely to occur, where, and when. This involves mapping, to show where such activities may occur, on the one hand, and identification, showing which individuals or groups may be involved or affected, on the other. Increasingly, the data feed comes from sources such as social media. For instance, if there is talk of going to bars and getting drunk, the GPS tags in the tweets indicate where trouble-spots may emerge, which can be mapped appropriately.

Imagine a scenario where, en route to an emergency call-out, officers use a smartphone browser to get access to a platform giving details that will help them to prepare for what they find at the scene. The platform has access to billions of publicly available commercial records as well as to criminal and social media information which it sorts and scores in seconds. An algorithm assigns a threat rating of green, yellow, or red, allowing officers to be forewarned about what they may find. The stakes are high. Such ratings will affect police calculations about the use of force, for instance.

Interest in 'big data policing' has expanded rapidly, especially in predictive policing. Allocating police resources may be done on the basis of such findings. Such systems are attractive to police departments keen to reduce their reliance on beat officers and to find new means of reducing operational costs and projecting an image of technological efficiency. And it makes sense to distinguish between the ways that police 'platforms' are emerging to make practical use of new data availability, and specifically 'predictive' techniques. Either way, data quality may be less than ideal, due to being incomplete, biased, or plain incorrect. This may produce results including false positives or negatives or the under-reporting of crime may represent crime rates inadequately.

And as some data comes from on-the-beat police reporting, subjective aspects are almost bound to appear in some cases.

Also, given the evidence that police activities can in many places be discriminatory in their outcomes, for instance disproportionately targeting members of minority groups, it is unsurprising when this also occurs using big data. The results of predictive policing are only ever as good as the data entered, which means that self-fulfilling prophecies can fuel a misplaced focus on, for instance, areas of urban disadvantage.

Problems arise in volatile environments, such as police work or national security, where the data may be gathered from situations that are ambiguous, or in which they already have negative or misleading connotations. So although 'algorithmic' policing sounds as if it is more accurate because it is based on complex data this does not make it less susceptible to error.

The social dimensions of algorithms are explored to good effect by researchers examining contemporary policing that show how, for example, already-existing institutional practices affect how the data are interpreted. The UK government's Centre for Data Ethics and Innovation commissioned a study, from which some findings were reported in 2019, showing how frequently algorithms themselves may be biased. People from lower socio-economic backgrounds may be algorithmically calculated to 'pose a greater risk' of criminal behaviour. But this is sometimes an effect of their coming into contact with public services more frequently, thus generating more data, to which police frequently have access.

Police will continue to upgrade their technological arsenals in coming years, and assuming that appropriate care is taken with the data, this can improve their service. However, much is required in terms of clarity, transparency, and accountability before *predictive* policing software is reliably ethical and so safe to use. At present, the jury is out on these methods, especially if crime rates are taken as a guide. Many factors affect such rates and isolating key ones is notoriously difficult.

Data-driven national security

The first decade of this century saw a decisive shift towards new data practices in state surveillance, seen in intelligence-gathering and monitoring. The twin threats of global terrorism and of cyber-attacks catalysed a search for new methods that is visible in the activities of the largest intelligence community in the world, the liberal-democratic 'Five Eyes' group of nations and especially within the NSA. The changes depend on the explosion of data availability from the exponential expansion of digital communications in the early 21st century.

To produce intelligence, big data is used together with machine learning and reliance on statistical techniques. The volume of big data is in fact just one aspect. The important thing is the capacity to search, aggregate, and cross-reference large datasets. The Five Eyes agencies ramped up their data quest especially around 2010–14. Data became the mantra of intelligence, with the aim of improving national security in an age of cyber-threats and exploding communications media. Global crime, violence, and terrorism are significant problems today, and many careful analysts struggle to capture key trends and detect threats.

However, it is still debatable how far the quality of the intelligence gleaned from data analytics is reliable enough for full use by security and intelligence agencies. Some say that abandoning old methods in favour of new may have negative consequences for individuals and groups, that in turn might exacerbate the problems they try to solve. There are limits to automation. Human involvement—especially from those who have a sense of history, politics, and law—in the process is vital for putting security threats in context, and this is jeopardized as greater weight is placed on algorithms and machines.

Within the Five Eyes, questions are raised about each others' practices, particularly over the question of how far the new data-based kinds of surveillance are adequate to the task. Some fear that too much faith is placed in the products of data analysis. Trust in technology and dependence on data are hallmarks of the big data mythology discussed by José van Dijck. As she says, 'Dataism presumes the objectivity of quantified methods as well as in the independence and integrity of institutions deploying these methods, whether corporate platforms, government agencies or academic researchers.'

Data-driven approaches shift from a logic based on targeting in search of causes, to a logic of bulk collection and correlations. Sometimes, the quest is for patterns pulled from 'raw data' rather than carefully testing hypotheses. Using machine learning, algorithms, and statistics, correlations may be generated when datasets are mined for patterns. From there one may move forward to prediction, rather than backward to explanation. The crucial skills are a statistical sense and the means to visualize data in order to interpret the patterns.

But the data gathered are still just a sample, selected for certain purposes with some specific end in view. These facts frame the data collected. Moreover, any information based on them still requires an understanding of context and knowledge of the security-surveillance background.

Surveillance makes visible the activities of certain individuals or groups such that, in the case of security intelligence, they may be assessed for their possible connections with criminal, violent, or terrorist activities. When there is a shift from targeted to bulk collection methods, different people become visible and, without extreme care, innocent people might mistakenly be viewed as suspects. This is because among other factors, the standards for individual suspicion were lowered after 9/11; new data practices can make some already marginalized or disadvantaged groups more vulnerable than others.

There are ways of handling the tension between the sorts of transparency required in other areas of democratic polity, and the limited information that can be shared by a security-intelligence agency. The key expectation is that such agencies be *accountable*, such that ordinary citizens can be reassured about the democratic commitments of such agencies. The UN prompted the establishment of an International Intelligence Oversight Forum in 2018 but not all agencies participate. The development of accountability practices lags behind new data developments. But that accountability is rightly demanded by citizens wanting reassurance that those agencies can be trusted.

Humanitarian aid

The global migrant crisis has reached epic proportions. In 2023, the UN estimated that the world contains 103 million 'forcibly displaced people'. Three-quarters of them are from Afghanistan, South Sudan, Syria, Ukraine, and Venezuela. In October 2022 fighting flared in North Kivu, in the Democratic Republic of the Congo. Nyiragongo territory now hosts 177,400 displaced people in two villages about 50 km from the conflict. They are uprooted from their land, their only source of subsistence.

For humanitarian agencies, such as the International Committee of the Red Cross (ICRC), the urgent challenge is to address issues of accommodation, sanitation, healthcare, drinking water, and food, here as in so many trouble spots especially in the global south. Such situations demand rapid and effective action, for which biometric registration—usually using fingerprints—is increasingly seen as a highly efficient tool. It is an agile means of accounting for who has received what assistance, or reconnecting families, and thus also for audit trails and accountability.

Biometric data are highly sensitive, creating a permanently identifiable record. For the EU, for instance, this marks them for special care. Bodies such as Privacy International have blown the whistle more than once on egregious uses of biometric data in humanitarian aid, making it an area of considerable controversy. But the ICRC developed a series of forward-looking policies to try to ensure that potential misuses would be minimized. Displaced and migrant people are right to worry that such details could be (mis)used, for instance by governments that obtain access to the data as a means of border control. Even the proper use of biometric data may be hard to justify. Restoring family links is a fairly straightforward and understandable use for the data, but increasing the efficiency of distribution of needed resources could be harder to defend, especially in organizations that have for a long time managed satisfactorily without such aids.

The ICRC has developed not only its own Data Protection principles but also produced a specific Biometrics Policy that speaks directly to matters such as how data-gathering is explained to those being given aid by the Red Cross, including how they can refuse to participate if they wish. Recipients of aid are given the dignity of recognition in the knowledge that the Red Cross actively endeavours to ensure that the data are used appropriately.

Big data in the real world

Carefully developed for specific purposes, data analytics, machine learning, and AI, not to mention biometrics, have great potential for the common good. But as our examples demonstrate, much care should be taken with developing them. Seen through a surveillance lens, the consequences of new data practices are often far from comforting. They do not necessarily work or work as advertised and when they do, they may exhibit features that call in question their enhancement of fairness, justice, or the common good.

Recall the earlier discussion of surveillance capitalism. Vulnerable groups often find their situations worsened. Real estate software may reduce access to suitable housing for those who most need it. Policing tactics can focus excessively on 'usual suspects', whether people or neighbourhoods. Medical diagnostic tools may be skewed by racial assumptions. And during a crisis such as the COVID-19 pandemic—as the World Health Organization warns—there is a constant temptation to see the situation as 'exceptional'. This leads easily to downplaying normal restrictions on surveillance.

For instance, automatic temperature-testing was used on passengers entering airports or contact-tracing apps, with varying degrees of success, were used to work out who might have been near someone infected by the virus. Automated temperature-testing in airports may be adopted as a public relations ploy. Apart from possibly contravening legal limits on personal data collection, temperature-testing on its own is an unreliable guide to infection. As for opt-in methods of contact-tracing using smartphones, they depend on public willingness to adopt them, as well as assuming that a whole population carries smartphones. Much sensitive data may be collected without solidly reliable results appearing.

While the three Vs mentioned earlier are important, one can add the V of 'vulnerability' because of increasing evidence of what political scientist Virginia Eubanks calls 'automated inequality' across a wide range of practices. Her research demonstrates that data-enhanced social sorting puts at greater risk certain already disadvantaged populations such as minority racialized groups, those without the resources or desire to own smartphones, people with disabilities, or single mothers.

All these aspects of surveillance capitalism are led by the market, even though government is close behind, both prompting development and benefiting from its products. But what if government took the lead in actively promoting scoring systems resembling surveillance capitalism? Many believe that in China, the same kinds of data generated elsewhere are used officially by the government to influence behaviour in ways that they hope will produce responsible citizens.

But it is not a unified, central government-led system. There are some local, municipal 'Social Credit' systems that combine data from employment, education, law enforcement, and social media use to create a 'trust score' to determine who is a truly reliable and loyal Chinese citizen. There are also commercial schemes, such as 'Sesame Credit' from Alibaba, but the rating and scoring criteria vary. They also have no connection with the blacklisting system, which can be checked on the Credit China website. The point of all these is to 'build trust'. Some citizens laud these systems, proud of their scores. High Sesame credit may resonate on dating apps, for instance.

When an initial plan for a government–corporate social credit system was rolled out in 2014, the government asked eight private companies to provide the systems and algorithms. In 2018, those companies were required by government to register with the People's Bank of China to create a citizens' credit scoring agency—'Baihang Credit'—as a public–private partnership.Thus in some Chinese towns and cities your citizen score may influence your future opportunities for getting a job, a loan, even getting a date. You also need a household residency permit (*hukou*) to enrol a child in a public school (private schools have their own criteria). The idea is to create a culture of 'sincerity'. Sounds good. What could go wrong?

To some, who believe that it could just go wrong, it seems to be a gamified loyalty system for nudging people into preferred behaviours and for leaving those with low scores out in the cold, meaning slower internet, restricted access to restaurants, clubs, international travel, insurance cover—the list goes on. That is, a sophisticated sorting system of inclusion and exclusion, orchestrated by government but powered by corporations.

Of course, the downside of incentivizing behaviours deemed loyal to the Chinese state is deliberately to discourage dissent. Citizen rights and privileges are likely to be denied to those whose scores fall below certain levels, especially when it comes to practising certain religious beliefs, posting political opinions at variance with the official line, or publicizing events that the authorities wish to hush up. However, such activities are proscribed anyway, without any 'scoring'. Indeed, known political dissent means no chance of train or air travel, or obtaining a passport. Certain ethnic and religious groups also attract rather more punitive surveillance, too. The largely Muslim Uyghur population in Xinjiang, north-west China, is monitored heavily and many have been detained in re-education centres. The development of 'gamified authoritarianism' is unlikely to feel like fun to them.

The Chinese case is of great interest and importance but in liberal democracies the state and the corporation still have somewhat different relationships. In such societies, the rule of law may be challenged in new ways by data-driven surveillance, especially when it is applied in areas such as policing, security, or elections. But what if such societies themselves adopt aspects of Chinese Social Credit?

Darwin, on Australia's north coast, invested in a 'safer territory' scheme, enabled by a 2018 law that gives law enforcement and security agencies potentially unlimited back-door access to communications technologies. Authorities can use people's phones to track them, erecting virtual fences that trigger an alert when a targeted individual crosses the line. Critics believe that what is advertised as 'switching on Darwin' is actually switching on aspects of Social Credit.

Much is in flux, especially as platforms increase their influence over both governments and populations. But what do we know about the populations themselves? In the next chapter, we dig deeper into the *culture* of surveillance in order to think further about the meaning and consequences our own everyday involvements in such surveillance.

Chapter 5
Surveillance culture: an everyday reality

A few days ago, I sat down for dinner with some new acquaintances in a restaurant. One of them opened the conversation with 'I understand you do surveillance studies—what is that?' As I responded, it quickly became clear that they were eager to discuss something that has become such an unavoidable part of taken-for-granted everyday life. They were concerned about companies collecting data to profile them and security agencies probing the lives of ordinary citizens. They questioned whether this surveillance should be allowed to happen. But they also spoke, ruefully, about their own involvement in surveillance through their smartphone and laptop use. How can we do otherwise? We depend on—even enjoy—these technologies. They felt the tensions.

What if I had been sharing a meal with friends in Hong Kong, Johannesburg, Paris, Tokyo, Buenos Aires, Bratislava, or Bangalore? Would they have asked the same questions or referred to the same experiences of surveillance? Well, yes and no. They would have darkened or brightened the banter with their own examples. The closeness of the Chinese superpower to Hong Kong, indelible memories of South African pass-books or of informers under the Argentinian dictatorship, or motifs from Indian spy movies or from computerized policing on the streets of Bangalore would add local inflection and colour to the conversation.

There is no single culture of surveillance, and a conversation in a medium-sized Ontario city would not be replicated across Canada, let alone the globe. There would be features in common, given the global character of surveillance developments, especially those relating to the internet and its platforms. But cultures of surveillance also form quite differently, depending on history, politics, and, well, culture. Maybe the Argentinians would have read Schweblin's surveillance novel, *Kentukis* (now in English, *Little Eyes*), or the Japanese would worry about the surveillance potential of Japan's 'Society 5.0' plans.

This chapter explores the realities of various 'cultures of surveillance'. How does our everyday experience of surveillance affect the way we see the world, and go about our activities? Have we been affected more than we know by living in a surveillance-saturated world?

Surveillance culture is inescapable

When we speak of surveillance as a part of everyday life, recognize the benefits of health monitoring, rely on our bank's digital fraud prevention capacity, comment on our own complicity in surveillance, monitor our peers, dismiss doubts about where our data ends up, or are perturbed about what the police or marketers do with those data, we give evidence that we have outlooks and experiences in common. This culture of surveillance is one in which our attitudes and activities are more and more attuned to surveillance. It's part of the landscape, an inescapable experience; familiar, unavoidable, commonplace, invisible. We depend on data in every sphere of life, and we think we know how to rate the risks, when to laugh off some challenge to privacy, and when to take a data breach very seriously.

After all, most organizations—schools, doctors' practices, libraries, banks, for instance—do surveillance by collecting personal data in order to help them intervene effectively in people's lives.

Surveillance definitely has some human benefits. Yet it has become increasingly hard to distinguish between the data practices of police, whom one might expect and even wish to do surveillance, and those of marketers, whose activities are not normally described as surveillant.

The apparent riskiness or randomness of everyday life makes such surveillance seem necessary to businesses and law enforcement. And the domestication of surveillance practices in daily life—think of face recognition, or self-monitoring for health or fitness on our devices—makes it more normal and taken for granted. In a surveillance culture, we get used to (or uneasy about) our daily lives being increasingly transparent not only to ourselves but also to unknown others.

Surveillance culture may be sensed through seeing online or media reports or perhaps through opinion polls or interviews but more likely through internet memes, movies, and novels such as the series *Black Mirror*, popular movies from a classic like *The Conversation* to thrillers like *Enemy of the State*, or, more recently, Joanna Kavenna's novel *Zed*.

Reading *Zed*, you have to put Orwell's concerns on one side. Not a government, but 'Beetle', a powerful technocratic corporation, oversees all, surveillantly. You can do nothing—and are nothing—without your smartwatch device, the beetleband, which identifies and entitles you. Whether for shopping or policing, Beetle devises the algorithms. Although not Beetle's fault, of course, if some algorithms don't work they are dumped in the Zed category, for being unpredictable. How human. Kavenna specializes in caustic irony. But her datafied society cannot cope with such dark humour.

While *Zed* and other artworks illuminate the 'culture of surveillance', the way that term is used here does not refer primarily to novels, films, music, or art. It speaks more to the ways that surveillance has become part of a whole way of life. How would an anthropologist see this?

Watching as a way of life

While watching is clearly a way of life for marketers, police, or security agents, in a culture of surveillance everyone ends up not only being watched, but also watching others. When employers check online profiles when interviewing job applicants or border security agents allegedly sometimes do the same when you show your passport, you sense that intimate aspects of your life are being scrutinized.

But how does this scrutiny differ from when you yourself check your preferred platform to find out more about someone you just met in a bar or when you perform an internet search on a neighbour? The answer, of course, is that employers and security agents represent powerful authorities who have access to your data, while you represent no one but yourself (even though in social media you are represented as part of a group and by your connections to others like you). However, power is still involved, if only of a more local and horizontal kind. The background check on your drinking companion may enable you to build a relationship; the scan of your neighbour may make you more wary. Social surveillance shares several features of large-scale, conventional surveillance.

Social media erodes the edges of social contexts and social roles, as media researcher Alice Marwick writes. This complicates knowing what exactly is private or public but makes social surveillance easier. Users strategically reveal, disclose, and conceal personal information to create connections with others and to tend social boundaries, managing their online personas. Power is still significant even though it is mainly individuals who are involved and there is also a reciprocal relationship as people look at each other's information, images, and videos. But this simply means that surveillance practices are domesticated—albeit unevenly across populations—in day-to-day life and interpersonal relationships.

As social media has spread, so platforms attract different kinds of users. Instagram's single, carefully presented identity contrasts, for example, with Tik Tok's more playful multiple identities. But what they have in common is that users post and message their friends continuously. They also use the platforms for finding out about others, both friends and strangers. This may seem far removed from the power associated with top-down surveillance, but power relations, of more interpersonal kinds, are still involved. When you know something about someone, that could be used to influence them—after all, people check on the tastes and proclivities of those they wish to date. On the other hand, the same tools may be used to shame or to disgrace others. A kind of power—to interpret, to give meaning to what is found—is present there, too.

Also, discovering data about others, particularly if they are in authority, may give you an advantage in certain situations. Police, or teachers, lose credibility if they are exposed as secret drinkers or petty criminals. The kinds of blurring and realigning of social differences that began in the 20th century with television continues in social media. On TV in the 1960s, children, for example, could for the first time watch adult lives in a new way, enabling them to reassess their own parents by comparing their family life with others'. In the 2020s, the internet offers opportunities to extend this in several ways.

On social media, those with privileged, especially influencer, status can dominate the platforms. Old contexts, such as status differences, may collapse, and new ones emerge, in a fluid fashion. The boundaries between one user and another fluctuate, as users reveal, disclose, or conceal information among their friends and followers and these create connections, seen in 'sharing', and exclusions, in 'de-friending' and worse.

From self-tracking to participatory surveillance

Even social surveillance and *sousveillance* do not exhaust the possibilities today. Focused, routine, and systematic watching may also be conducted on oneself, for instance to check one's fitness or health, using wearable devices. Often called 'self-tracking', this phenomenon is very popular in some contexts and produces quantities of data of interest not only to keep-fit enthusiasts or weight-watchers, but also to medical, pharmaceutical, and healthcare agencies and organizations if they obtain access to the data. As noted earlier, surveillance is a multi-directional way of making others visible and even of making ourselves visible to ourselves and others.

This approach to surveillance moves beyond merely *being seen* to consider how, in ordinary everyday life, *seeing others* has taken on some fresh characteristics in a surveillance culture. The fact that you are seen in new, mediated ways encourages us to see the world differently. The presence of surveillance cameras, for instance, makes a difference to how people perceive social situations. As soon as you see the little lens on the wall or ceiling, in the post office, your workplace, the cinema, or the fitness centre you may start to wonder what images are being captured and why.

Communication scholar Jonathan Finn sees surveillance as a social practice based on the human desire to see and be seen. In this sense, it's an aesthetic concept, visible in advertising, but drained of any hint that surveillance might be ambiguous or even dangerous in some contexts. He also suggests that, in visual culture, surveillance—especially cameras—may be used to emphasize the reality or veracity of some state of affairs. For instance, in *The Truman Show* or *CSI*, surveillance lends authoritative weight to the dubious idea that the camera tells it like it is, and enables a form of participation in public life. Similarly, smartphone photos taken at an incident make their owners not just witnesses but agents. You have to be ready for action; surveillance is also a bystander duty.

Seen these ways, surveillance is not merely what people see but what they do. It is a practice calling for participation. Everyday engagement with surveillance is not just complying with the red-light camera or making online privacy trade-offs but is participation in surveillance, weaving it more closely into our daily lives. For Finn, surveillance has 'morphed from a technology to a way of seeing and a way of being'.

Finn harks back to earlier writers Susan Sontag and John Berger, who discussed ways that, in the 19th and 20th centuries, photographs fostered new ways of seeing and how, for example, memory no longer works the same way. The mental image of an event is replaced by a photo into which we inject meaning. And if that was true of photos, or, later, public space video cameras, which are Finn's focus, how much more is it relevant to a smartphone-saturated world?

Such effects—that lead to changes in the ways people use online platforms—are now common aspects of surveillance culture. Once, the idea of such effects was virtually ignored in law courts. How could one build a case on something so vague? But law scholar Jonathon Penney demonstrated that the use of online information is affected significantly by such publicity. Many users self-censor their searches, avoiding certain websites, steering clear of some conversations, or hesitating to share content. Government surveillance online is a disincentive to participate 'as normal'. Young people and women are more likely than other groups to be disturbed, but also to take steps to defend themselves.

Paradoxically, though, apparently opposite tendencies also exist. Many social media users want to be visible, to be seen. Even before social media became as culturally central as it is today, some observers noted that older technologies such as webcams drew out some playful and enjoyable kinds of practice.

From the earliest days of webcams, people would perform for others, seeking audiences for their show. Back in the mid-1990s a female college student set up a webcam called 'Jennicam' in her dorm that broadcast her daily activities to any and all. In a sense, she was the first life-streamer. Researcher Hille Koskela called this 'empowering exhibitionism'. More recently, people speak of 'youtubers' or 'social media influencers'. The public-spirited climate change activist Greta Thunberg is a classic example—from her debut in 2018, as a 15-year-old, she knew how to use Instagram and Twitter to great effect. She has nearly 15 million followers.

Today such activities are commonplace, indeed magnified by social media, where many feel affirmed and empowered through cultivating their online personae. Surveillance, in this sense, so far from being malign and sinister, may be thoroughly enjoyable, desirable, and fun. It is also possible that the same people may be both chilled *and* cheered by their online involvement.

Part of surveillance culture, then, may involve holding on to somewhat contrary imaginaries and practices at the same time. We may enjoy the fun of our enhanced visibility to surveilling others while still being at least half-aware that something else is also happening with our images and data. It may be that the decision is consciously made to continue despite the downsides. Or that different approaches are taken depending on other factors. For instance, wariness about certain effects may prompt a decision to use encryption for some routine activities such as writing emails. The more users realize that every interaction increases their visibility to corporate others, rather than just to friends or followers, the more circumspect they may become.

From checking to stalking to vigilantism

It is one thing to consider the playfulness and empowerment involved in some online communications and games. It is another to think about how users make watching part of their way of life, now using new technologies. The dominant surveillance culture, seen for instance in platforms and providers, actively promotes and rewards people that watch each other. Accumulating likes and followers brings benefits and business profits. So what happens to social relationships when this becomes widespread and a taken-for-granted practice?

Different kinds of watching are seen on a spectrum, varying in intensity from 'checking out', to stalking, to vigilantism. Each of these is a new practice, historically speaking, but each also becomes everyday very quickly. The fluidity of changing patterns of online behaviour means both that it is hard to know what is the current situation and difficult to remember what went on previously. For example, there was a time when the word 'stalking' was being used loosely to describe some fairly innocuous 'checking out' of others' details online. With growing awareness of the scourge of online of sexual abuse, however, descriptive language becomes more precise.

Needless to say, some kinds of online research are definitely not welcome to other users, particularly if they edge towards the intrusive or abusive behaviour dubbed cyberstalking. Such harassment may happen to an individual, a group, or an organization and may run from annoying attention—or worse, sexual predation—to making false accusations or slandering the entity in question. It is different from trolling, which is making offensive or provocative online posts.

Cyberstalking is persistent and unwanted contact that leads to fear or at least distress. Its perpetrator may well be someone who has difficulty relating to others and spends a lot of time on the internet, becoming fixated on some individual or group in an unhealthy way. This is of little comfort to the victims of cyberstalking.

Recent years have seen the rise of 'stalkerware', marketed particularly as parental software control or employee monitoring. This is consumer spyware, produced by companies similar to those who sell private surveillance services to governments. Such apps can be secretly installed on a 'target device' in order to monitor the activities and communications of the child or employee concerned. The likelihood of such spyware causing harm is obvious.

More self-conscious, legal, and sometimes collective ways of doing surveillance on others are crowd-sourced policing—often seen by participants as public-spirited—and digital vigilantism, often seen as a public nuisance. The one believes that they are capable of policing and indeed will work with police under some circumstances. The other feels that public policing is inadequate and takes things into their own hands. Is this the 'weaponizing of visibility'? Such vigilantes try to hold fellow-citizens accountable through online naming and shaming or worse.

For instance, in 2015 Walter James Palmer endured global outrage for killing a much-loved lion in Zimbabwe. Activists around the world attacked him through social media. Either form may be viewed as a problem for police, not least because they involve public naming and shaming. They are surveillance in the sense that personal details are collected and shared in a systematic and specific way to contribute to some perceived emergency or social crisis.

In the 6 January 2021 riot at the US Capitol in Washington, DC, police were quick to get access to cellphone tower data in the hope of prosecuting perpetrators. Some of the rioters even incriminated themselves by taking selfies and live-streaming video while in action. Meanwhile, well-meaning observers set up an Instagram site for crowd-sourcing the process of identifying miscreants from publicly available video, encouraged by authorities. For instance, the FBI tweeted photo-collages of rioters' faces, asking the public for 'tips and digital media' to aid their task. Time honoured distinctions between tasks get blurred in times of crisis, and varieties of surveillance that might not otherwise be tolerated—such as police use of facial recognition technology and crowd-sourcing private identification—may be normalized.

In a 2017 case in Singapore, bank employees were wrongly identified as a young couple who had been caught on a viral video, bullying an elderly man in the Toa Payoh hawker centre. As well as publicly shaming innocent people, the bank in question was also threatened with boycotts. The misidentified woman described the ordeal as 'emotional and scary'—dependent as it was on assumptions made from a poor-quality video. Such occurrences are all-too-frequent aspects of the weaponizing of visibility, enabled by a participatory surveillance culture.

The privacy paradox

As participation in social media took hold as an everyday reality, a curious phenomenon emerged. Users were quite aware that large, impersonal, platforms craved access to sensitive, revealing personal data for their own purposes. They expressed worry about it, but seemed to act inconsistently by disclosing information anyway. This quickly became known as the privacy paradox, which assumes that people do care more about their personal data than they appear to and maybe that better controls should be available within those media. Exploring this apparent paradox opens another window onto surveillance culture.

Early versions of the privacy paradox hinted that young people especially tend to share information online fairly freely in ever-increasing quantities, either thinking that platforms are relatively private or that they could manage their data themselves. But from the second decade of the century it dawned on users that the corporations in question were hardly altruistic, vacuuming those data for profit and influence. It seems that for many, the 'paradox' settled into the belief that the authenticity of self-presentation was more significant than worrying about whatever metadata were collected about them.

But things are much more complex than the 'paradox' suggests. Consider the view that users often exhibit an implicit trust in datafication, its experts, and its results. A subtle suggestion suffuses surveillance culture, that the swelling amount of circulating data is basically beneficial, that the platforms require it to improve their service and can be trusted to handle it on users' behalf. Such views encourage users to relax their guard over 'their' personal data with at least limited confidence that releasing it is in a good cause.

However, other users of social media are often aware of the ways that their data are gathered and analysed by the platforms they use but resign themselves to the data collection because they can see no alternative. They sometimes make a trade-off in order to retain access. It is said that 'I've read the Terms of Service' is the biggest lie on the internet. This may sound cynical, but certainly not ignorant or mindlessly compliant. Users aspire to control the flow of information but realize that privacy settings are weak, unclear, and change frequently. Users' consequent frustration may lead to apathy or self-censorship. The businesses they deal with depend on users sharing as much as possible and thus have no incentive to make user nudging and steering any clearer or stronger.

But what if the paradox depends on an illusion of control, as others argue? In this case, the quest for privacy may be likened to that for safety by using car seatbelts. Such restraints do not necessarily make things safer in every case, because research shows that people drive less carefully when wearing them. Online, users may be given an illusion of control—through corporate promises, for instance—that actually reduces their guard, inducing incautious sharing of personal or other sensitive details.

Not only are different views held by users-in-general, such differences also reflect variations in factors such as age, gender, race, and class. Research by the American Pew Center think tank in Germany, Australia, and Japan shows that older users tend to be more circumspect than younger when it comes to consigning their data to social media. They will either avoid social media or hesitate longer before sharing data. The platform-of-choice will also make a difference to how much data is collected. For instance, in the USA more women than men use Pinterest, and Hispanics in the USA and Latin America are heavier users of WhatsApp than other groups.

Cultural cues and clues

Culture is about codes and symbols, about what are appropriate modes of relating with each other, with institutions, things, and places. How contemporary life is depicted, maybe mirrored, in art, film, music, and novels is a way of parsing cultural cues and clues. Contemporary cultural products, especially TV series, films, internet memes, and even art exhibitions and the daily news help to inform our understandings of surveillance culture.

Notions such as visibility, transparency, privacy, exposure, and vulnerability come vividly to life in drama and comedy, in text and image. And of course, memorable literary phrases or figures from films themselves become part of everyday cultural experience. A radio commentator refers to some government scheme as 'Orwellian' and we immediately know what she has in mind and how she expects listeners to hear the news.

In the West, the 20th century obtained its most memorable metaphors from Orwell, though Aldous Huxley—*Brave New World*—had some highly pertinent things to say about surveillance as well. Surveillance could be achieved in soft ways; for Huxley it was the drug, *soma*, but this could translate today into the beguiling smoothness of consumer surveillance. Novelist Franz Kafka also offers tropes for today's surveillance. In *The Trial* the victim of surveillance has no idea why he is targeted, who is watching him, or what are the consequences of this eerie shadowing. Today this speaks to the inscrutability of data surveillance, its slippery uncertainties.

But it is Orwell to whom public commentary frequently falls back. Who can forget the image of Big Brother staring accusingly down from the telescreen on the hapless citizens who had nowhere to hide, or the twisted language of political messaging in official 'doublespeak'? While some read Orwell as a prophet railing against the state socialisms of Iron Curtain countries of Eastern Europe, others caught the irony that political and technological potentials within Western states also meant that Big Brother was not so distant from 'liberal democracies'. Orwell's name became synonymous with criticizing and dissenting from the totalitarian tendencies lurking within any society.

George Orwell's work offers some marvellous metaphors and some profound insights into surveillance. Big Brother's malevolent gaze is decidedly top-down; Winston Smith's fear and loathing of it is visceral. But after more than 70 years, with tectonic technological shifts and the now massive dependence on the consumer realm of surveillance, Orwell's direct relevance for today's conditions is waning.

Many today have learnt to love Big Brother, or have at least made their peace with him. In a consumer context, surveillance may be associated with personal performance, with our capacity to discover a social media audience and with it new possibilities for instant communication and the swift gratification of felt needs for everything from sports results to ride-share programmes. Nonetheless, Orwell's commitment to the possibility of free, full, and 'decent' social relationships is still discernible in these latter-day depictions of a much different world. Big Brother's association with a reality TV show rather than a dystopian novel could easily dull our senses.

Tellingly, one of the most compelling pieces of 21st-century surveillance fiction, Dave Eggers's *The Circle*, itself mimics Orwell's style even though, as literary critic Peter Marks sagely observes, 'Big Data stands in for Big Brother today.' The Circle's corporate headquarters is in California, where this tech company has swallowed up all the other big players in its embrace. Versions of the privacy paradox, for instance, are aired in the novel, as are numerous other pressing problems associated with the internet, social media, and surveillance. A key theme is transparency, one of the urgent goals of the company and one that brings both wry humour and poignant pathos to the plot. The protagonist, Mae, a 20-something eager new employee at the Circle, strives to be fully transparent while also struggling painfully to find moments to herself.

Much of her time is spent franticallytapping away at her keyboard as she attempts to make her quota and to maintain her ranking as a fully participating Circle member. At the Circle, updated Orwell-type slogans are mantras of this cool environment, among them: Sharing is Caring. Maybe so, but for Mae, sharing is also indispensable for scoring because when she does so, others respond, raising her ranking.

It is hard to miss Eggers's message and it speaks, again, to both the corporate and the consumer aspects of surveillance culture today. And because this corporation believes that it can govern better than dated democracies, *The Circle* also probes corporate contributions to political surveillance. The brilliant 2021 sequel, *The Every*, finds Mae in a senior role, but where the political impact of the superseding company is even greater. Eggers's scathing critique of high-tech dominance is a clarion call. It signals the potential human toll of wall-to-wall surveillance. Behind the dystopian text Eggers is gasping for more humane air, all but smothered by data-powered corporate goals.

Such literary contributions help open our eyes to the ways that surveillance cultures form and novels like Eggers's or Joanna Kavenna's *Zed* are echoed in the scholarly treatments of organizational and consumer culture. Watching workers *is* increasingly intensive and intimate in many settings where dataveillance tracks daily activities, with a view to manipulating behaviours. The trend is towards using manifold data for imperceptible surveillance. Practices like peer-to-peer evaluation and watching one's colleagues' performances help to modify workplace cultures. And as workplace surveillance analyst Kirstie Ball suggests, when surveillance goes beyond performance monitoring and extends to the bodies and minds of employees, new questions must be asked.

Equally, in the consumer sphere, popular culture's commentaries and caricatures of the scrutinized consumer have academic analogues. Kirstie Ball and David Murakami Wood pinpoint the role of 'brandscapes' of control in today's marketing toolkit. The brand is meant to reassure and excite the consumer with a familiar product. But by it, consumers are coded in terms of their desires and their place within a network of consuming possibilities. Thus their buying behaviours can be analysed in order to set them up emotionally for seduction. In this way, consumers are both 'exhilarated and exploited'. Thus cultural tropes intertwine with more scientific approaches to surveillance today.

Troubling tactics

It would be easy to conclude from some readings of *The Circle*, *Zed*, or *Black Mirror* that the die is cast. The hegemony of the global surveillance-industrial complex is all but complete and it is only a matter of time until everyone is fully in the thrall of the swirling data vortex. The surveillance strategies of the powerful, in whatever country or region, create irresistible force-fields against which fighting is futile. Why would anyone wish to war against the consumerist corporations when they offer such tantalizing and tempting distractions? The dominant surveillance culture that idolizes new technologies, craves new markets, and wraps itself in a beguiling 'sharing economy' has as a key goal, pleasing the consumer.

The mistake here is to assume that the dominant culture is the only one, that no residual refusal exists from previous cultures or that emerging cultures have neither a distinguishable identity nor potential political clout. Social thinker Michel de Certeau, for example, shows that looking only at *strategies* of power—the case of large corporations—is inadequate. We also need to examine the *tactics* of everyday negotiation with large commercial, consumer entities, seen for example in the different approaches to data-sharing among users.

The strategies of large-scale social media platforms are clear, to monetize data. They help to shape surveillance culture, but they may also be challenged by the tactics of users. Ball and Murakami Wood hint that contesting the 'brandscapes' world is unlikely to be a social movement as much as a 'fractured' and uncoordinated process. Perhaps seen in events such as large-scale deactivating of social media accounts after data scandals.

Jonathan Finn asks, 'What are the impacts on social relations in a culture that actively promotes and rewards citizens surveilling each other?' What he has in mind is camera surveillance, in which ordinary people become both producers and consumers. But today the same questions must also be asked of social imaginaries and practices of device, social media, and internet use. Finn's comments are poignantly pertinent here, too: living in a surveillance culture 'requires a self-reflective look at our own willingness and desire to watch, record and display our lives and the lives of others'.

Chapter 6

Questioning surveillance: critical probes

The largest biometric registration system in the world was developed in India. The astonishing Aadhaar system aims to enrol all 1.4 billion citizens within a single digital system not only for identification purposes but also to enable participation in the digital economy. The concept was born in 2006 and launched, creating the Unique Identification Authority of India, in 2009. The appealing idea was that this would alleviate conditions for India's most impoverished people, offering the chance to demonstrate their claims on the state. Government campaigning has encouraged close to full participation in Aadhaar and many have marvelled at the technical progress towards completion. Socio-economic rights are being advanced and, to many, the single system has been shown to favour good governance (Figure 5).

After the COVID-19 pandemic broke in 2020, not only was the Indian response itself dependent on Aadhaar, but the idea of replicating Aadhaar-style digital identities for countries in Africa and elsewhere was widely promoted. Digital social identities were seen as key ways of dealing with population-level crises such as COVID-19, as well as offering a basis for later developments such as vaccination certificates. Indeed, the UN Economic Commission for Africa Digital Centre of Excellence pointed out that '500 million Africans do not have a foundational ID from which they can fully transact business, [or] get benefits from the

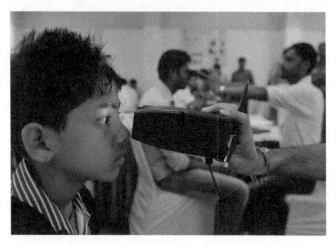

5. Biometric scanning for Aadhaar.

government…' The pandemic offered the perfect opportunity to take strides towards what other countries have had for decades—an ID system entitling their citizens to social security.

Aadhaar was used to expand the Public Distribution System of food-based welfare, with its one-nation-one-ration-card (ONORC), and to ensure that vulnerable migrant workers could also benefit despite not having a fixed address. Direct cash transfers were also enabled to reach other at-risk groups, especially low-income or unemployed women. As Aadhaar numbers were integrated with mobile phone numbers, this facilitated the administration of vaccinations, and the issuing of vaccination certificates with unique QR codes for each person in real time.

A report from Azim Premji University suggests that more could be done, however. Aadhaar can identify the poorest people but falters at the point of actually supporting the most distressed and vulnerable. Also, the system may work in certain states—cities and rural areas—but there are disparities of coverage, especially in farming communities depending on, for instance, landless workers.

These kinds of discrepancies fuelled dissatisfaction long before COVID. The Hindi word Aadhaar means 'foundation', the basis, in other words, of Indian National Identification and, critics fear, the development of a relatively unaccountable multi-purpose surveillance infrastructure. The scheme has been questioned from the start by a variety of players, for the abuse of power that might occur within such a massive system of connected databases, the potential invasion of citizen privacy, and the prospect of a more tiered society.

Fears focus on the claim that Aadhaar facilitates the creation of a surveillance state with unprecedented access to personal details relating to health, welfare, education, socio-economic standing, religion, and more. In 2017 and 2018, for example, a significant group of lawyers petitioned the Supreme Court of India to dismantle Aadhaar as being incompatible with democracy and the rule of law, on which the Indian Constitution is founded.

The Aadhaar system is promoted for its convenience; one ID number that can be used for many purposes. But the same one-stop ID can also be problematic. From an administrative viewpoint it is the visible face of a complex system of identity control and management. It helps to make India's vast population more governable. Proponents argue that biometric identification is one of the most reliable systems available, thus limiting fraud. But such reliability is questioned, both by scientists and by human rights groups, due to the possibilities of misidentification. Lawyers argue that the fault lines are many, and controversies show no sign of abating.

Identification systems are basic to surveillance that is intended to lead to appropriate intervention in the lives of specific individuals or groups, as seen earlier in the discussion of Western welfare states. In countries with existing digital networks that embrace the majority of citizens, identification is enabled in multiple ways. The advantages of a single system have to be weighed against the possible risks, especially those of negative discrimination against certain population groups. In India this affects Muslims and Dalits—once called 'untouchables'—in particular and other minorities in general. But Aadhaar has built-in official categories for redress for such caste inequalities. In democratic societies, including India, such matters can be publicly debated and resolved through the rule of law, in ways that avoid unequal treatment for different groups.

The ambivalence of surveillance—care or control (or both)—has been illustrated consistently through this book. Surveillance can be very beneficial in some contexts, but the very techniques on which it depends, and the corporate and governmental powers that promote it, also make it questionable. Debates about surveillance are commonplace and occur at every level, from local to global. Questions have to be faced, not merely by academic analysts but by policy-makers, governments, educators, and people encountering surveillance in everyday life. The critical probes of this chapter emerge from philosophical and theoretical ideas as well as from personal experiences and shared misgivings of those affected by surveillance.

This chapter examines different ways of questioning surveillance, starting with privacy, but does so with a view to finding widely agreed grounds for surveillance critique and contest, not for working against all surveillance itself. Ethical perspectives are of the essence here, but not only ethics. Without the political, ethics may easily be subverted or used as a substitute for seeking solid change. Without the ethical, the political may lose its purpose.

Weighing surveillance

Everyone is affected by surveillance, all are also implicated, and there are avenues for all to query surveillance. In a sense, surveillance is now not merely state-down as in the Orwellian model, or horizontal as in 'social surveillance'. It is also diagonal, as French political sociologist Didier Bigo insists, in the sense that surveillance by powerful entities both public and private builds on voluntarily disclosed personal information as ordinary users engage in their own online surveillance of friends and others on privately owned company platforms. The terrain of conflicts and struggles over personal data and the limits of both business and government data-gathering and data-sharing is one that is here for the foreseeable future. And part of the struggle occurs on the very same internet and platforms as produce many surveillance challenges in the first place.

Many social media users are unruffled about how platforms treat them. They are not dupes of an oppressive system; they make conscious choices, to live with whatever the platforms do, for the sake of convenience or other gains. On the other hand, these same users may become aware of how platforms manipulate our data in hope of managing our behaviour, and may respond by deleting their subscriptions, or sharing their negative experiences publicly. They may also choose to join less surveillant platforms. And they may join forces with others or with organizations pressing platforms to address perceived problems or to demand regulations to govern their activities.

Such responses to surveillance are far from new. Back in the 1970s, 220 workers went on strike over the widespread introduction of video cameras at the Puretex knitting company in Toronto (Figure 6). The (mainly immigrant) women were outraged; cameras even appeared in the washrooms, but were switched off the for the men's shifts. Workers sang a song composed, in Italian, for the strike:

> We want to make some progress
> But the cameras must come down
> We do not like it, Signore Padrone
> We are not Sophia Loren.

6. Puretex strikers, 1978.

The three-month protest won the day and the cameras came down. The arbitrator of the dispute commented that controversy over electronic surveillance 'attests to people's instinctive identification of its fundamentally anti-human character'. Similar sporadic pushback against CCTV has occurred in other contexts. Indeed, in general, unwarranted or inappropriate workplace surveillance has often been met with successful resistance. This is especially true for manufacturing workers around the world.

More than four decades later, surveillance cameras still exist in many workplaces and they are sometimes less visible to employees—and during work-from-home due to the pandemic of 2020 to 2022, many workers were obliged to keep their computer cameras on during business hours. But they have also been joined in some places by practices such as monitoring all email, internet, and telephone use with or without the workers' explicit knowledge. Not only that, practices such as *combining* customer and worker surveillance—seen, for instance, in the fast-fashion industry where cashier metrics and biometric timekeeping are added to video surveillance—creates further worker insecurity and precariousness. There is less face-to-face interaction *and* more digital surveillance to cope with. Researcher Madison van Oort has shown that this *also* affects women, and black women in particular, in certain geographical locations, as they now have to struggle with 'emotional labour' of the newer surveillance as well.

Surveillance affects not only management-and-labour frictions but also ones of gender and felt indignity. Everyday human life is touched by surveillance, in this view. What would have been appropriate watching at Puretex? Management stated that they were responding to employee theft in this case. And what was inappropriate? The male management monitoring female workers? The scale of the coverage? The use of cameras at all? Today workplace surveillance touches human lives in deep ways, where inequalities, uncertainties, and emotional struggles appear together because of the simultaneous multiple contexts in which surveillance is experienced. Contexts and mediating technologies may change. But each highlights the need for critique, contest, and the quest for equitable solutions.

Some have been fought for and made available. Australia has a Workplace Surveillance Act. Data protection laws in many countries may be used, at least in a limited fashion. Trade union laws can also be applied to working conditions, including the right to protest certain modes of surveillance.

In today's digital era, just about every kind of disadvantage and indignity, whether it refers to social standing, economic viability, racialized, gendered, or religious discrimination, can be mediated if not magnified by surveillance. This is largely the fruit of surveillance capitalism's rise to prominence, using everyday data to score and rate everyone in ways that produce invisible and ineluctable rankings. Today's social sorting mechanisms affect all lives, all the time. Being able to participate in society as peers is a basic human aspiration. As the Puretex arbitrator implied, the issues raised by surveillance today touch on our very humanness.

Surveillance under scrutiny

In the West, privacy has long been thought of as a key antidote to surveillance, seen negatively, because intimate information—names, addresses, phone numbers, insurance IDs—about personal lives is at risk of unwanted exposure. However, it is far less obvious that what is known by organizations about individuals is 'intimate'; data about the time, origin, and recipient of a message, a call, a post, for example, seems trivial, incidental, and even innocuous. But much can be gleaned from knowing where someone was, when, or whose is the most-called number of some individual. The larger questions today are about how people are categorized based on the collection and analysis of such seemingly trivial data. How carefully are the data collected and curated? How are the algorithms constructed and are they biased? How are the data used, by whom, and with what authority?

This is one reason why ethics and politics are important. Surveillance is not intrinsically conducive to human flourishing but nor is it inherently destructive of it. In some circumstances and contexts surveillance may be highly appropriate and in others it is emphatically not. The ethical question is deciding which is which. The ethical desire to do the right thing must extend into exploring how to do it, which is political. No analysis of surveillance is neutral because surveillance itself is not neutral.

Privacy against surveillance?

A defining moment in the story of modern privacy occurred back in 1890 when US lawyers Samuel Warren and Louis Brandeis published an article promoting 'The Right to Privacy' in the *Harvard Law Review*. What had previously been loosely covered by a range of legal instruments could, they argued, be pulled together into a general right that 'modern enterprise and invention' were threatening to undermine.

A few years later, when a photograph of 16-year-old Abigail Robertson was printed on a bag of flour without her consent and with the poor pun, 'flour of the family', this 'right' was tested. Why could this young woman not be protected from others using her image for profit? Although the court decided against the minority legal opinion, within a few years this new right was increasingly accepted in civil law in a number of US states.

A mid-20th-century stage of what might be seen as an ongoing political struggle over privacy was seen in a birth control case, *Griswold v Connecticut*, in 1965, when the denial of privacy was viewed as violating the constitution of the USA. As historian Sarah Igo shows, it also connected privacy with wider debates about women's rights. A new television series, *American Family*, also created ripples about privacy in the 1970s because a Santa Barbara family allowed the cameras into their home to film them live for a 12-week series. What, if any, were the limits to such exposure? Around the same time (1967) legal scholar Alan Westin opined that privacy should be thought of as 'control of our information', an idea that soon became a significant force in the politics of surveillance.

However, the question was often framed as one of *personal* privacy, as indeed it is taken to be in the US Fourth Amendment, where people have a right to 'be secure in the persons, houses, papers and effects, against unreasonable searches and seizures…' and where the person is taken to be individual. As personal information was collected more extensively by both government and commercial agencies in the later 20th century, to be stored in searchable databases and matched against other records, so the question of privacy took on a wider political meaning. Fears of a return to authoritarian government led to calls for seeing privacy in relation to democratic participation and the common good.

In the West, Orwell and Huxley saw the governmental potential of surveillance in the 1930s and 1940s. But now the pressure was on to find fresh ways of expanding the debate over privacy to demonstrate its value, not only to individuals, but to society as a whole. Privacy cannot sensibly be lifted out of its social context. Privacy is not an abstract right, or something to be contrasted with social relationships, so much as something we negotiate with others in everyday life. Westin allowed himself to focus on the flows of information, thus deflecting attention from their role in real-life social relationships.

Reducing privacy to personal concerns pits the individual against data-gathering agencies and seeks to balance their mutual interests. In this case, it is all too easy to see how so-called 'individual' concerns can be marginalized by appeals to security or convenience. Far better to check first that the surveillance should be allowed at all, and then offer data protection to ensure that safeguards are in place. This is because, as politics academic Priscilla Regan argues, privacy is a *common* value, shared by others, a *public* value, in any democratic system, and a *collective* value, required in a world where technological and market forces would otherwise make many individuals very vulnerable.

Debates over privacy will continue, especially as legal scholars struggle to find ways of updating older laws to match the challenges of surveillance capitalism. For example, legal thinker Anuj Puri puts things starkly: '...in the age of Big Data Analytics, privacy as a right can no longer be exercised meaningfully individually'. Referring to COVID-19 apps, Puri goes on to say that, apart from strictly limited exceptions in 'grave emergencies, there is no moral justification for round-the clock surveillance of an individual's existence...'. Because we are seen by surveillance as members of groups, it is our *similarities*, not our distinguishing features, that need protection. He concludes that a 'Group Right to Privacy' is required to address the themes discussed in this book.

Limits of privacy

As we have seen, surveillance scholars often acknowledge the importance of privacy, but many still question the usefulness, adequacy, and relevance of privacy as a singular antidote to surveillance today. Why? Privacy is narrow, rooted in liberal ideas of subjectivity and property, worries mainly about 'intrusion' and 'invasion' into people's lives, leans towards individual rights, varies historically and culturally, and does not focus sufficiently on the discriminatory social sorting that amplifies inequalities. As well, to assure others that privacy protections are 'in place' may be window-dressing, obscuring what actually happens to personal data. Privacy, many argue, must give way to—or at least be complemented by—other ways of addressing the politics of surveillance.

To take just one of these factors, historical and cultural variation in understanding privacy is extensive and makes for difficulty agreeing what is the real problem. Thinking of the Western world, privacy has gone through phases. It was *public* life that was valued, for instance, in the 18th-century French Enlightenment, but *private* life that later came to be championed as a bourgeois right in 19th-century Europe. As such, appeals to privacy also tended to be associated with property and gender; the 'Englishman's home is his castle'.

But international understandings of privacy vary markedly. Privacy may be understood in bodily, communicational, informational, and territorial terms, but there is considerable variation of how privacy in these dimensions is valued. While North American countries along with France and Japan consider informational privacy to be paramount, other countries think that different kinds of privacy are more important. Broadly speaking, Brazil values bodily privacy most, while Spain, Hungary, and China put communicational privacy in first place. Many cultural, political, and historical factors help to account for this. But given the global character of the technical systems, it is vital that agreement be found that respects and accounts for such differences.

More than one gauntlet has been thrown down that acknowledges these variations but questions some faulty assumptions about how to frame and to govern privacy. It has shown great resilience as a concept, regime, policy instrument, and as a shorthand for civil society activism. Others note privacy's role, but baulk at seeing privacy as *the organizing frame* for counterposing surveillance. It is possible to use privacy to ensure that, for example, proper procedures are observed to ensure that employees have at least some protections from undue management scrutiny in the workplace, but this will hardly limit the spread of surveillance.

Whichever position one takes, a vital dimension of privacy goes beyond individualist readings to consider the social value of privacy. Surveillance threatens not just 'my privacy' but society itself. Privacy, insist some, creates important spaces for deliberation within democracy. This does not mean that the private and the public are completely separate spheres. A key danger here, as feminist critiques of privacy show, is that the family be seen as part of the private world, somehow shut off from palpably public concerns such as domestic abuse. Public and private are interconnected and people invariably live their lives between the two.

Public and private contexts are also critical. Privacy is not merely about controlling the flow of personal information but also about social relationships in all their complexity and variation. It is not enough to claim that we should be able to control the flows of our communication—even if that were possible. The same information might be thought of very differently in different contexts. On a public street or park there may be some justification for surveillance cameras, but it is imperative that you know you are watched. Notice should be given as fair warning that cameras are present. What counts as 'personal information' really does depend on the context. Name, address, date of birth, social insurance and phone numbers no longer operate alone. People are identified algorithmically—for instance in facial recognition technologies—such that all kinds of data may play into 'personal information'.

Privacy can also be thought of in ways that reflect the classic Western liberal self, in which autonomy is sacrosanct. Yet that self is not a 'given'. It emerges as humans develop *in relation with others*. Many say that freedom from unwanted or excessive surveillance is vital for informed and reflective citizenship. Equally, such freedom is essential for innovation, for the creativity and playfulness without which important changes cannot occur. People do need protection when commercial and government bodies seek only fixed, predictable, and transparent persons and groups. Those same people learn self-determination as they try to manage the boundaries between different contexts of information flow and that process, too, deserves protection.

Questioning privacy and data

Surveillance has always encountered problems of social acceptability, even in earlier times when most relationships were more direct and face-to-face. But further difficulties arise with modern bureaucratic and technological developments that tend towards the impersonal, and now with profiles based on data fragments and the increasing automation of consequential categorizing that today often includes AI. The world of policing, for example, has become more and more dependent on police as 'knowledge workers', dependent on abstract digital data. The use of information systems and digital technologies in policing has intensified progressively since the 1990s. Such increasingly impersonal developments include Live Facial Recognition (LFR) technologies, trialled, for example, by the London Metropolitan Police between 2016 and 2019.

Police in London mounted a camera on a van equipped with a control centre to monitor the feed and be in touch with officers on the ground. Large events such as sports or protests could be watched this way. Biometric data from the live feed was compared with watch-lists. Researchers Peter Fussey and Daragh Murray observed and analysed this from a human rights standpoint. One key finding was that the LFR paid inadequate attention to equality and diversity issues. The Association for Computing Machinery in New York has argued that facial recognition technology should not be used due to its 'clear bias based on ethnic, racial, gender and other human characteristics'.

In Europe, the primary legal language for questioning surveillance is 'data protection'. Based on earlier developments, such as 'Fair Information Practices', and 'Digital Rights', 'privacy' features less prominently than in North America. Data privacy speaks to what those who have lawfully collected information might do with it and how far you can retain and use it. But data protection safeguards data from unlawful access by unauthorized parties. The question of personal data includes privacy but puts the focus on appropriate ways of handling data. As many examples in this book have shown, while some 'personal' data may be thought of as 'private' in some sense, much data circulates without generating particular worries for those whose data is used, especially data that originates from consumer transactions and attention.

Many who maintain that privacy is important insist nonetheless that it be thought of in social, contextual ways. Cases such as LFR cry out not only for data protection but also for a careful questioning of how policing is conducted. This is also true of predictive policing. The idea that officers might be able to intervene pre-emptively depends on data analysis of an algorithmic kind that makes assumptions about different kinds of neighbourhoods and types of people.

Perils of social sorting

As far back as the 1601 English Poor Law, ways were found not only of distinguishing populations in terms of sheer need, but also of differentiating between 'deserving' and 'undeserving' poor. Put crudely, criteria such as age, disability, or sickness suggested that it was not the claimant's fault that they were poor. If they were feckless or work-shy, on the other hand, they were to blame for their condition. Such bureaucratic classifications clearly make judgements that have impacts on the population, especially if little is known by welfare recipients of the criteria by which they receive help. These processes are a basis for social sorting.

In the case of legislating to reduce poverty, surveillant data-gathering still makes some similar judgements today. Sophisticated algorithms guided by complex criteria, usually unavailable and likely unintelligible to welfare recipients, end up informing decisions that often have very unequal outcomes. Not only that, hiring practices that use credit scores create a poverty cycle. As mathematician Cathy O'Neil says, 'if you can't get a job because of your credit record, that record will likely get worse, making it even harder to land work'. Debt, she observes, should not be framed as a moral issue. Plenty of trustworthy, hardworking people lose jobs and fall into debt when companies fail or employers cut costs, especially during a crisis such as a global pandemic.

Judgements of different kinds have consequences, elsewhere, especially in historical colonial and post-colonial situations, where arbitrary population data classifications created to ease the burden of rule-at-a-distance may have devastating effects. For example, the Belgian administrative categories of Hutu, Tutsi, and Twa meant the difference between life and death in the Rwandan genocide in 1994 (Figure 7). Identification is basic to surveillance, and population records that offer ways of categorizing 'different'

7. An ID card that cost this woman her life in Rwanda in 1994.

groups also offer the means of watching them and intervening in their lives in ways that relate to the categories. In Israel, the mid-20th-century administrative division between Jewish Israeli, Arab Israeli, and Palestinian is today decisive for life chances and participation in Israel and Palestine. As Elia Zureik shows, these distinctions can make all the difference in how one is 'seen', and thus represented and treated, by surveillance in Israel, the West Bank, and Gaza.

A crucial way of questioning surveillance is to ask how it functions as social sorting in different sites. To classify in this sense is to allocate individuals to categories to, as it were, put them in their proper place. In earlier periods of history 'proper places' were more fixed, in terms of location (as well as in other ways), but those locations became a means of sorting on a large scale with the emergence of the modern nation-state. In today's context, each citizen's 'place' morphs into a (perhaps more changeable) social, economic, and political classification depending on educational achievement, disposable income, or voting habits, for example. As surveillance becomes ever more complex, enabled by digital technologies, so sorting becomes more fluid as categories in one domain may reappear in another or as ranking processes engender categorial fluctuation over time.

Oscar Gandy's work on 'discriminatory technology' was mentioned in Chapter 2. Database marketing—also known as 'Customer Relationship Management'—is about collecting customer data to understand their needs and to enable personalized communication about products and services, and is governed by strict privacy laws in many countries. Gandy likened the process to an emergency triage in a hospital where a nurse checks arriving patients. Their assessment involves classifying according to certain criteria and ranking in order of the seriousness of their condition. This sorting-by-category has clear outcomes for each patient. In an earlier marketing context the sorting was primarily by 'geodemographic segmentation', which divides populations by postcode (zipcode) on the assumption that neighbourhoods tend to attract similar kinds of people. But this produces a system of uneven access to the consumer marketplace for goods and services because some postcode populations are more desirable marketing targets.

Manifold developments have been built on database marketing in the early 21st century. The most significant have to do with the explosion of data from user-generated content, as social media data emerged as a source of great profit. So-called big data practices expanded to work with such data while AI and machine learning added new techniques for predicting and nudging customer 'needs'. But the capacity to track the movements of consumers—and others—in real time, through their phones, also took marketing surveillance to another level, with finer-grained profiles. Location analytics companies using phone data can vividly 'visualize' consumers' movements from store to bar to gym and so forth, creating movement as well as life-cycle images. A company that connects people who need rides with others offering them clearly benefits from such location analytics, as do the riders.

Marketing distinctions between consumers with varying 'lifetime values' to the corporation and revealing patterns of movement create uneven commercial playing fields. And the platform process of ranking such customers for varying treatment, using big data analytics in a plethora of situations, shows not only the pervasiveness but also the mutating character of social sorting. Add to this the ever-increasing 'smartness' of devices and systems that connect our lives through appliances, vehicles, and buildings, and their connectedness through cloud computing, and we see not only 'convenience', but also conspicuousness to multiple corporations aiming to shape our lifestyles, and, indeed, our lives. Thus many kinds of inequality become automated, especially with the growth of surveillance capitalism.

For those already disadvantaged or deprived, the sorting process is felt even more intensely. The poor, especially those of colour in certain countries, are further marginalized and neglected in this process. Political scientist Virginia Eubanks argues that 'While poorhouses have been physically demolished, their legacy remains alive and well in the automated decision-making systems that encage and entrap today's poor.' At least poorhouse overseers had to confront the flesh-and-blood families needing care. Now many welfare workers sit before their screens using software created by engineers.

To automate may seem to create efficiencies, but how it fails shows another side. A 6-year-old 'lively, sunny, stubborn girl', Sophie, in Indiana, received a letter informing her that her Medicaid benefits—which kept her alive—would be stopped very soon for her 'failure to cooperate'. This was the automated response to her parents' minor error, whose resilience and social capital, thankfully, helped them correct the situation. Her dad, reflecting on this, observed that people with lesser skills might not have managed this. Automating the process, suggests Eubanks, may further distance those deciding on the allocation of social housing and other state help, and the recipients of such help, with the outcome of a weakening sense of societal shared responsibility for eradicating poverty.

Surveillance as exposure

A big question, from our discussion so far, is, what is distinctive about *today's* surveillance? Only when we have a handle on that will we be able to comment on the variety of ways in which it can be approached and evaluated. Many theorists, such as Foucault, have useful insights, but as we noted earlier, the kind of 'seeing' involved in today's surveillance is very partial. James Scott's 'seeing like a state', for instance, focuses on how citizens are *made visible* to the state, which may be extended to how employees are *made visible* to employers, or to how consumers are *made visible* to corporations. That is to say, we are constantly *exposed* to many kinds of gaze that are seldom interested in 'us' so much as in specific and discrete aspects of our lives. That begs at least two further questions: how are we exposed? and by whom?

If one examines surveillance from the perspective of the subject, then it becomes clear that more than behavioural or statistical elements are important. As Kirstie Ball observes, much surveillance aims to obtain access to subjective aspects of life: feelings, dispositions, outlooks. In a call centre, for instance, she shows how employees are encouraged to 'smile down the phone' and to self-motivate to hit targets, all while their conversations are recorded for 'quality control'. They are performing, no less than some might do when they realize they're under a surveillance camera.

While some are exposed by police, the tax office, or the boss, much of our exposure today relates to the pleasurable pursuits of online life. And while surveillance capitalism is clearly engaged in the task of enticing us to expose ourselves, this is not experienced by most people in a negative fashion. It's often felt to be enjoyable, and many, especially on social media, *want* to be seen. Indeed, some even leave their phones on at night so that no opportunity is missed. This is closer to Huxley's *soma* drug than Orwell's Big Brother. As Bernard Harcourt observes in his book *Exposed: Desire and Disobedience in the Digital Age*, so far from repressing our desires, today's surveillance exploits them. Indeed, it often aims to create and feed addiction to being seen.

So who is surveilling? Orwell's worry was state surveillance. But clearly, surveillance is now a common mode of finding out about people's everyday lives, engaged in by most organizations, but especially by platform businesses seeking to discover as much as possible about consumers. And those very data are readily sought, simultaneously, by police departments, intelligence agencies, and the like, to bolster their practices. Legal scholar Harcourt colourfully describes this ever-changing surveilling entity as an 'oligopoliptic octopus'. Even in China, often read negatively as the epitome of 'state surveillance', government agencies depend on the self-exposure of consumers and citizens—rewarding the latter for their loyalty.

States are still active, of course, as is capitalism—hence 'surveillance capitalism', which is a very powerful force, straddling the two. And clearly, market-driven surveillance turns our own productive activity against us, for ends that are not ours. Shoshana Zuboff would agree with this but stops short of blaming capitalism per se. For her, new forms of accumulation, based on data extraction, threaten the very humanity of its subjects and destroy the social fabric, including, importantly, democracy. Her target is ascendant 'rogue companies', not capitalism itself.

So if surveillance today relates largely to desire, and if the agencies of surveillance are manifold, not just the old holders of power, then how is surveillance appropriately questioned? This is examined further in the final chapter, but one comment is called for here. If surveillance is about how aspects of our lives are made visible, or exposed, then that process deserves careful examination. Everyday exposure portrays us in particular ways, which is then how we are represented to any others who have access to the profile. And on that basis, our case will be handled—as consumers, patients, students, workers, citizens, or whatever. An important dimension of surveillance critique lies right here; querying those data themselves, along with their role in representing and treating us.

Essentials of surveillance critique

There is no one 'correct' analytical, ethical, or political perspective for questioning surveillance but there are several possible approaches, many of which may be complementary. As I see it, any approach that has integrity will emphasize trusting relationships, care for the Other (meaning especially population groups that are already disadvantaged), along with benchmarks such as purpose, proportionality, and other principles. These are used widely—in 35 member countries of the OECD—as essential ways of safeguarding personal data.

Here's an example of how disadvantage may be embedded in the *way* we're seen. In the medical sphere some diagnostic software used for monitoring patients may be biased against certain racialized groups. Increasingly popular among time-strapped medics are apps that enable doctors, using their phones, to check what medical journals say while making a live diagnosis. Though potentially a useful and life-saving tool, the algorithms driving the databases behind such technology sometimes incorporate biases. For example, race and ethnicity relate to disease in complex and contradictory ways, which can be damagingly represented on the doctor's screen. Any such bias, of course, deserves exposure and demands modifications to software tools. It may also require doctors to be trained *not* to put too much confidence in such systems and to ensure that second opinions are sought routinely.

The need to ask the right questions about surveillance has never been greater. To corporations and government departments you are what you buy, drive, where you go for fun, online or otherwise, and your personal story of health, education, and employment, contained in those digital files. These place you in their categories, guiding decisions about your prospects, your life chances, your choices. However, it is important to recall that while particular softwares and algorithms—such as those in medical diagnostic apps—help to produce certain kinds of inequalities, simply tweaking the technology will not solve the problem. Data discrimination cannot be decoupled from larger systems of institutionalized unfairness. Technology mediates the particular problem but it is part of a large, all-too-familiar, family of problems.

This is why it is vital to explore and expose the part played by the political economy of surveillance. Today's world is increasingly infused by surveillance capitalism that affects every area of life. This includes, especially today, democratic practices that are frequently crucial for ensuring some protection for those whose social position is already weak. Information flows are all too often controlled by large commercial companies whose priorities in customizing news delivery may include sensationalist content that can, in some cases, drive engagement over accuracy or civic values. If democracy is eroded, for example by excluding some groups such as recent immigrants from participation through microtargeting voters, then the appropriateness of that surveillance should be ethically questioned.

Surveillance raises some crucial questions of trust, self-determination, and responsibility. Trust between persons may be damaged if it turns out that one party has been watching the other, say, through a keyhole, blind, or curtain, without the latter's knowledge or consent. Not surprising, then, on a macroscopic scale, that after the intelligence-gathering revelations of 2013 many were outraged that the NSA has 'inadvertent' access to information about ordinary American citizens—not to mention citizens of other countries.

On the other hand, surveillance may be a way of discovering whether or not someone can be trusted in the first place. Think of nannycams, for example, where inappropriate treatment of an infant, as seen on a video without the knowledge or consent of the nanny, may lead to a termination of employment. The impact of surveillance on trust raises profound questions that demand to be faced.

After all, however intangible it sounds, trust is still the vital glue holding society together. It is basic to social relationships and therefore its erosion by certain kinds of surveillance raises profoundly ethical and political questions. Data breaches, particularly at giant corporations or in government departments, immediately damage trust.

And when intelligence agencies claim that the metadata they collect and analyse is relatively innocuous when in fact it relates to the kinds of things sought by private detectives—where and when a contact was made and for how long, for instance—once again, trust is the casualty. The ability to trust others' activities and words is critical for satisfactory social relations, including those between individuals and organizations of all kinds.

Likewise, self-determination is an important ethical concept, in this case seen as the ability of individuals to present themselves and, more broadly, live in the manner that they choose, with freedom and responsibility. In the classic case of the Panopticon, the idea was to ensure compliance through the constant threat of repercussions following some breach of expected conduct to control behaviour. Public space video surveillance, often thought to have deterrent qualities, operates in the same way, on the assumption that those in view of cameras will observe the local laws and expectations for fear of discovery. Such disciplinary control could even be seen in the case of social media, where social surveillance encourages particular kinds of self-presentation calibrated to a behavioural norm expected within that platform's self-disciplining performance of roles.

Because social sorting is so central to how surveillance works, it is hardly surprising, once the objectives of the system are understood, that citizens, consumers, travellers, and employees would want to know first if such a system is treating them fairly. The cause may not be recognized by some as 'surveillance', but the effect is all too apparent, and as these systems aim at total coverage, the effects will increasingly be universal if nothing slows or stops their progress.

Curiously, each of these concerns also speaks clearly to concerns expressed in fiction by George Orwell, Margaret Atwood, and Joanna Kavenna—the threat of surveillance overreach. Accountable modes of governing, and of the civic involvement of all in political processes, are a necessary antidote to the democracy-undermining effects of some surveillance. As one examines the political economy of surveillance alongside the ways of creating compliance and muting dissent in control societies, the challenges to democracy become plain.

This is as true in India, with its amazing but deeply controversial Aadhaar system, as anywhere. How this fits with aspirations to better manage the Indian economy through digital networks and thus ensure a place among future global players while simultaneously addressing the needs of the most marginalized is a challenge accepted by its creators and supporters. Alongside each are profound desires for a distinctive democracy in India and, due to its colonial past, a legal system that privileges privacy. Together, they contribute further to the challenges of shaping and confronting surveillance in India today.

Chapter 7
Encountering surveillance: what to do?

In the 21st century, while everyday surveillance is often relatively benign and socially beneficial, the accelerating shift to the digital, propelled by governments and corporations, has prompted a rapidly growing chorus of voices expressing concern about the evident downsides of several kinds of surveillance. Everything from personal unease about where sensitive data can travel to public outcry against egregious data-handling activities makes everyone more conscious of, and sometimes more cautious about, surveillance. But because data, algorithms, and organizational protocols are so arcane and invisible to non-expert citizens, and because state and corporate actors are so powerful, the big question is 'what to do?' This chapter considers some strategies, from personal protection to public participation, in both citizen and consumer spheres.

This book stressed from the start that when we speak of surveillance, we're considering something that has an enormous and growing presence today. It's a reality built into the very structure of today's world, helping to soften distinctions between economic, political, and social affairs that were once thought to be distinct. But we have also seen that everyday human lives also play into the world of surveillance in various ways. Creative and active ways of responding to and, when needed, resisting inappropriate or unfair surveillance, are worth noting.

From private troubles to public issues

The difficulties of living in a world of smartphone-and-video-camera surveillance vary considerably, as do the range of ways to deal with them. In everyday life there are many uncertainties about surveillance. Is my young daughter endangered by my posting pictures of her online? What exactly is my boss monitoring as I work remotely? The seemingly trivial turns seriously troubling, especially when lifted from its original context. Inappropriate or compromising comments or photos, or details about race, age, religion, pregnancy, or disability, can affect life chances and choices.

That is straightforward and easy to grasp. But the fact that your drugstore discount card collects data unique to you about your purchases hardly seems worth a second thought until you know that it becomes part of a profile that could well be sold to other companies—insurance, private clinics, pharmaceutical firms—that may rate your chances of contracting some disease and contact you to sell some service or, more awkwardly, refuse to offer benefits because your case is construed as too risky.

When confronted with some dubious surveillance, you may make an instinctive move to resist by hiding, avoiding, blocking, or otherwise trying to neutralize the gaze. Even if it is only to turn away from the camera, smudge the digit being fingerprinted, or use a shared code in an online message, these are ordinary, mundane ways of resistance or at least of non-compliance. These are individual responses, but they should not be ignored.

From reading some sources you would be forgiven for concluding that the big story of surveillance is one of limits on freedom, constraints on living, and hegemonic control. Michel Foucault's work sometimes gives this impression, but he also insists that 'where there is power, there is resistance'. French intellectual

Michel de Certeau takes this further. How, he asks, do people resist being reduced to the 'grid of discipline'? He urges that we spend time considering '…what popular procedures…manipulate the mechanisms of discipline and conform to them only in order to evade them'.

It may be encouraging when you discover that you are not alone in facing a negative experience of surveillance. The realization that many others are in the same situation can turn a personal problem into a public issue. One can ask the department or business about the problem or lodge a complaint with a privacy or data protection official. To bring questions to appropriate authorities yields opportunities for more collaborative approaches.

A strategic spectrum

For one example of everyday resistance that turned into a public—indeed a global—issue, Edward Snowden's exploits are worth noting. Several factors were important to Snowden's success. A loyal American citizen, with a family background in military service, he chose to work in security surveillance. However, while working as a regular NSA contractor, he realized that certain practices added up to inappropriate targeting of US citizens. This is an example of confronting surveillance by state authorities.

On several occasions Snowden felt obliged to question his superiors about what seemed to be 'mass surveillance'. Not getting any responses, over many months, he decided to find a way to go public. He chose a risky route of copying classified data, lifting only those that would not damage US security interests. He then made a calculated choice to call key journalists, which ensured he would find a ready audience for his discoveries. Each element made possible his disclosure of NSA overreach and unaccountability.

Of course, not everyone is involved in national security-related surveillance and very few have Snowden's opportunities. Furthermore, some take the view that Snowden's own course of action was inappropriate. But anyone working for any organization will themselves use data or find that their data are used to monitor their work and progress. You may not be the target of some egregious data breach or data-gathering expedition, but opportunities will doubtless arise to raise questions about and suggest alternatives to present practices.

Parents can ask why their children need so many cameras in school; students and faculty can ask why the university must gather so much data on students; police officers can question the attempts at crime prediction rather than having more direct contact with the local community. Opportunities will vary by context, of course—marketing employees, for example, may find it tricky to persuade employers that they can manage with less data. One doesn't have to be a celebrity whistleblower to be a dependable truth-teller.

Raising awareness

In 2002 Japan rolled out a computerized national ID system called Juki-net, intended to enrol all 126 million citizens. Weeks before, a major opinion poll showed that 86 per cent were fearful of data leaks and the improper use of personal data. Citizens rallied in the streets to protest, ripping up the government papers that demanded data for Juki-net. 'I don't especially enjoy being called by a number,' complained truck driver Yasuyoshi Ban. Mayors and municipal assemblies around the country objected so strongly that on the roll-out day, 4.1 million citizens were missing from the data system.

Some sued the government for invasion of privacy. By 2006 the Osaka High Court declared that Juki-net infringed privacy rights by insisting on the participation of dissenters. Eventually judicial appeal was made to the Japanese Constitution, claiming that Juki-net infringed on rights to informational self-determination enshrined in Article 13. Although the Supreme Court struck down that claim, these events helped to build suspicion of government surveillance that belies the stereotype of Japanese citizens as orderly and conformist.

The massive machinery of Juki-net still exists in central and municipal government buildings, used mainly for pensions, not as a centralized multi-purpose ID system. Public opposition thus succeeded, although a new 'My Number System' was created in 2016, seemingly similar to Juki-net. In order to obtain citizen buy-in, central government is proposing to make healthcare access dependent on My Number.

Private troubles become public issues when some means of awareness-raising, group-mobilizing, and protest-catalysing becomes possible. This occurs in a variety of ways. Other national ID proposals, for instance, have foundered due to protest. In the late 1980s, an 'Australia Card' was proposed as a means of enhancing citizenship and rationalizing dispersed databases. Many Australians felt that such a system would be an unnecessary threat to their independence and freedom. One young Australian journalist saw the ID card as a threat to democracy itself, and led a campaign against unaccountable government surveillance.

That reporter helped to galvanize a coalition of groups that contributed to scrapping the scheme and later to launching a surveillance watchdog, Privacy International (PI). It provides information and valuable reports on surveillance in many countries. Twenty years later in 2010, when a similar scheme was proposed in the UK, PI was among the groups lobbying against that ID system, in conjunction with a high-profile campaign called

NO2ID. Commentators argue about how decisive NO2ID was in defeating the UK ID scheme, but the movement certainly contributed to the victory of those who objected to it on the grounds that it would facilitate pointless and perilous surveillance.

On a smaller scale, some surveillance cameras in public spaces can create controversy. A ring of cameras that read licence plates appeared around a predominantly Muslim area of Birmingham, UK, in 2010. They monitored everyone driving in or out of the area, under the apparent auspices of a community policing initiative. However, when *The Guardian* newspaper revealed that it was a central government anti-terrorist strategy, shock, consternation, and anger broke out within the local community. Locals enhanced the cameras with signs stating, 'You are now entering a police state.' The legality of the cameras was questioned and police and the city council were obliged to apologize, backtrack, cover, and finally withdraw the cameras (Figure 8).

8. 'Bagged' CCTV cameras; Sparkbrook 2010.

From citizens to consumers

Growing consumer awareness also fuels dissatisfaction as customers discover how their sensitive data are being used. Opportunities may arise for pushback. In 2018 São Paulo's subway system introduced 'interactive doors' at three stations on the ViaQuatro Yellow Line. These doors included screens displaying customer information and also advertising. But the doors also contained lenses and sensors that maintained a count of passengers at different times and also watched for facial expressions of surprise, dissatisfaction, happiness, and emotional neutrality. They also estimated the age and gender of passengers by the screens.

However, the Brazilian Institute for Consumer Protection—IDEC—along with LAVITS, an academic surveillance studies network with links to NGOs, launched a civil lawsuit against ViaQuatro. Digital rights lawyer Rafael Zanatta objected that passengers had not given consent and were not notified about the existence of the surveillance. ViaQuatro was obliged to disable the sensors and lenses embedded in the doors.

What these examples show is that the perceived threat of increased surveillance may prompt opposition from various quarters; from citizens and consumers. In the consumer realm, things may be more complex, especially as corporations are often more nimble or adroit in their evasive or rebranding efforts, but here too, canny customers may voice concerns.

Tactical and technical responses

In extreme circumstances, such as the ongoing protests from 2016 against the loss of democratic freedoms occurring in Hong Kong, 'digital resistance' takes fresh forms. To evade surveillance, protesters set up an independent phone network, not connected to the internet, used more secure browsers, used encrypted systems such as Tor or a VPN, signed up for Protonmail email accounts, and installed the encrypted messaging app Signal. They also used tactics such as covering their ID cards in aluminium foil and leaving their phones at home during a protest.

While everyday responses to surveillance are understandable and sometimes quite effective, people often ask if there is more that they can do, at a technical level, to protect themselves from negative aspects of surveillance. There are many valuable anti-malware and protective systems available today but, more importantly, a number of initiatives to help the public, especially younger people, to act prudently online. Some, such as the EU/Council of Europe Digital Resistance programme, aims to educate high school students in careful and responsible use of the internet, which includes surveillance awareness.

Just protecting *oneself* has limits. For a start, installing software to protect laptops, tablets, or phones often favours those with technical expertise to actually make the changes. They also often have associated costs, which may be prohibitive to some. Market 'solutions' may have genuine benefits, but many insist that a better way is to demand protection for all. Groups such as the Algorithmic Justice League do just that, working to make AI more equitable and accountable. But many technical and market offerings keep the conversation at the level of 'personal troubles' rather than 'public issues'. The latter approaches also assume—realistically—surveillance will continue to be a feature of our lives for the foreseeable future.

Pressure points

In 2009, two energetic young Polish lawyers, Katarzyna Szymielewicz and Małgorzata Szumańska, along with some friends, got together in response to what they felt was a rapidly growing surveillance society. They created 'Fundacja Panoptykon' in Warsaw to protect freedom and human dignity in the context of growing surveillance in commercial or security contexts. Their aim is to keep surveillance policies and practices in public hands, with democratically determined goals. They see some benefits of surveillance, such as personalized service, but worry that even this can be manipulative. Today the outfit is a public watchdog and educational unit with long-term strategic goals.

The past 20–30 years have seen a rapid international growth and diversity among groups opposed to surveillance overreach. In the northern hemisphere, bodies such as the Electronic Frontier Foundation (EFF), Electronic Privacy Information Center (EPIC), and Privacy International (PI) are well known. But there are also Civil Liberties and Human Rights groups that are concerned about confronting surveillance as one among many issues they address. These include the International Network of Civil Liberties Organizations (INCLO) and Human Rights Watch. In addition there are regional groups, worldwide, that have central interests in combating unwanted surveillance and others whose remit is general but includes surveillance concerns, such as Open Media in Canada or CIPESA in Africa.

Although they provide important modes of confronting surveillance in their own right, many groups concerned with surveillance have a larger remit—to promote better policies, modes of regulation, and law. Though this may sound pedestrian, or even outdated, remember that in most countries governments still retain the ability to rein in corporations and even national security agencies and police departments. This is crucial. Seeking national and international modes of addressing the global explosion of surveillance is a vital and robust way of engaging the politics of surveillance. Such begins with updating older privacy and data protection regulation in specific countries and advances towards fuller quests for appropriate data governance on an international level.

The rapid rise of surveillance in many African countries, from Ethiopia in the north to South Africa in the far south, offers many examples of each dimension, the structural and the active. For a decade and more, both Chinese and, especially, American companies have been actively selling surveillance equipment, including to African government and policing departments. For instance, Huawei sold $126 million worth of CCTV equipment to police to combat crime in Kampala, Uganda, in 2019. Civil society groups made claims that their facial recognition capacity was being used to check on government critics in several African countries.

American interests have been prominent in South Africa, and elsewhere, for many decades, but since 1994, US exports of digital technologies and then of big data techniques, AI, and centralized cloud computing have also swelled surveillance capacities.

The African Digital Rights Network (ADRN) published a report in 2021 warning that the influx of surveillance equipment, often used by governments to track political opposition, amounts to a dangerous 'digital authoritarianism'. The ADRN recommends restricting the import of tracking technologies and dismantling laws, under an anti-terrorism rubric, that permit citizen surveillance. But this focus on *state* surveillance underplays the role of global corporations in the global south, which governments woo to buttress everything from bureaucracies to education. In South Africa, apartheid critic Archbishop Desmond Tutu joined others who insisted that giving people access to free and open software is a viable alternative. This was officially encouraged, but only briefly. Elsewhere, the idea of a 'digital commons' is promoted, playing the same role of placing the means of access in decentralized hands.

From privacy laws to 'digital citizens'

Legal instruments to curb unnecessary, inappropriate, excessive, and illegal surveillance have been developed slowly since the late

19th century, expanding in later 20th-century computerization. Today, such privacy and data protection laws are the backbone of governmental efforts to curtail and govern surveillance. Based on the notion that citizens have rights respecting personal data, they represent a steady and persistent means of regulating surveillance, affecting governmental, corporate, and law enforcement activities. Not only are such laws valued for their intrinsic protections, they also act as an important vehicle for other basic democratic rights such as freedom of assembly, speech, belief, and protection from discrimination.

Data breaches, subtle cyber-warfare, and state surveillance overreach are not merely vague threats; they occur with increasing regularity. Their effects on many vulnerable populations are considerable, and they menace both democracy and public trust. The European Union made a very promising start in 2016 with its General Data Protection Regulation. But these are also matters for groups such as the G20 to address with some alacrity and resolve. Or do we have to wait for what some call the 'Data Chernobyl' to occur before such matters are taken seriously?

But what if the users themselves, roused by campaigns like #deletefacebook, began a concerted effort to rein in and redirect such behemoths? As political scientist Colin Bennett shows, resistance to surveillance in the shape of privacy campaigns has never had the cachet or the unity of, say, the environmental movement. But is it possible, given what is now known about the highly surveillant *normal working data practices* of large online platforms, that such social media amplified flare-ups could spark just such larger resistance? The 2020s, which have seen an explosion of pandemic-related surveillance, may be the moment for such campaigns.

Many well-informed privacy advocates and activists from civil society have learned to use significant media, including artistic, dramatic, and musical performances, and privacy and data protection agencies around the world have become a necessary part of new technology developments including surveillance. But in the end, while much has been done to regulate surveillance, the results are piecemeal, with all too often temporary victories. A coherent, international movement has yet to emerge.

In 2012, a Declaration of Internet Freedom was signed by many prominent figures in the name of a free and open internet. It includes privacy: to protect everyone's ability to control how their data and devices are used. People such as Laura Poitras, who made *CitizenFour*, the film on Edward Snowden, are signatories, and so are those associated with the internet's early years, such as Vincent Cerf (USA) or Tim Berners-Lee (UK), international dissidents such as Ai Weiwei (China), groups such as Amnesty International, and a number of senior professors at leading universities.

Are these a new breed of 'citizen-subjects'? Social scientists Engin Isin and Evelyn Ruppert argue that such citizens are not only subject *to power* in the sense, say, that those under surveillance may be said to be, they are also subjects *of power* who carry responsibilities. They may at times suffer at the hands of the law—think of the decentralized international 'hacktivist' group, Anonymous—but the point is that they are making *claims* about rights, to internet freedom, including freedom from unnecessary, disproportionate, or illegal surveillance by government or corporations.

Unfortunately, digital rights people do not always speak of 'citizenship', but, rather, reduce these to the problems of 'individuals'. *Citizens* should be subjects and agents of such rights, especially when surveillance is the main focus of internet rights.

To capitulate to the common conclusion that we are incapable of contesting surveillance is to deny some crucial human capacities. A range of responses does exist. The issues raised by surveillance have to be approached in diverse ways. One can ask questions, make complaints on one's own, or enlist the help of relevant organizations and join movements that are committed to reducing or abolishing the kinds of surveillance that are unnecessary, overreaching, or illegal. There are technical, educational, activist, advocacy, and legal approaches that can tackle surveillance at local, national, or global and international levels. Pursuing digital citizenship is far from futile.

But this still leaves big questions unanswered: in what ways do resisting or reining in surveillance serve the common good? How far may surveillance itself have humanly beneficial results? At the end of the day, surely the quest should be not merely for reducing possible harms, but for positively promoting social justice, the common good, and human flourishing—all crucial political pursuits. So to what kinds of surveillance futures might we look?

Surveillance futures

Can we predict what will happen in the future? Can we assume that responsibly run surveillance agencies will lead the way such that processes of data justice, self-regulation, and adherence to legal regulation become routine? Or will surveillance continue to develop as some suggest, like the 'Wild West'?

Those anxious about surveillance ask, will our every movement, right down to eye and head movements, be tracked? In the effort to build a 'Metaverse', immersive virtual reality environments will follow these micro-movements. Marketers promise useful and enjoyable outcomes, but few comment on the potential for extracting more highly sensitive data.

Will children—like some pets or domestic animals—be implanted with microchips at birth? Will corporations take over more government functions, using data analysis and prediction to ensure efficiency? How far will AI be permitted to decide policing and legal choices, based on surveillance data?

The more sanguine reassure the rest, asserting that current checks and balances in democratic societies will be sufficient to stem the growth of rogue data-handling in government. And that any worries about what companies do with data are minor compared with the gains in efficiency and convenience experienced by customers.

Talk of surveillance is often muddied by dire dystopias, futuristic fantasies, promotional promises and reassurances, and the assumptions that technological solutions are best or that technologies work as intended. Distractions also include conspiracy theories and digital dread. But we cannot predict the future.

The world of novels and films favours futurism, of course. Understandably, people are fascinated by and fearful for the future and a common feature is the fallout from technological changes. For instance, the movie *Gattaca* tells a story of genetic surveillance in which one's social worth depends on having the right genetic inheritance. However gripping the movie, and however well it has been researched, such films serve only to stretch our imaginations, and perhaps warn of potential pitfalls.

There are multiple futures. Colombia's future won't be the same as Cameroon's or Canada's. Different paths depend on different histories, for example, of authoritarian government, free-market economies, or colonial settlement. Also, some major players, such as India or China, travel in their own distinctive directions to digital surveillance futures. Some common features, such as public–private partnerships and the outsourcing of government functions to private corporations, or the spread of surveillance capitalism, work differently in the global south and the global north. WhatsApp or ride-share platforms such as Uber, Lyft, or Grab are used in different ways in different regions even though the basic infrastructures are similar.

However, we can speak of observable trends, and also of undesirable and avoidable futures in the world of surveillance and of key elements that we may wish to hold on to as today's surveillance trends unfold ever more rapidly around us. Among these, the notion that human flourishing—peace, social justice, and the common good—should be paramount, offers some significant guidelines.

Surveillance and human flourishing

What do the issues explored in this book mean for the future? The most urgent questions have to do with trust in data, its escalating collection, multiplex analysis, and hugely diverse uses. In the 1930s the poet T. S. Eliot asked about the 'wisdom we have lost in knowledge' and the 'knowledge we have lost in information'. What he did not ask—the question was scarcely relevant then—is where is the information we have lost in data?

Eliot's deeper point concerned the human quest for wisdom. What happens when we lose sight of wisdom in the rush to embrace the latest data solution, the newest source of profit, the Midas touch for growth? Eliot hints at a hierarchy of value, with wisdom at the apex, followed by knowledge, and information. And now, I propose, data, on the ground floor. However, the hierarchy only makes sense if one is concerned with practical choices of what truly has value for life.

What if 'human flourishing' was the goal within which our hopes and fears for surveillance find a coherent context? Such flourishing might include several components. Social trust, for instance, includes the imperative for protecting privacy, in its several dimensions. Today, 'data justice', the quest of fairness in how people are 'seen', represented, and treated by data, would have to feature, too, especially related to poverty, gender, and ethnicity. And what about the demand that digital rights be established, linked to the need for democratic participation in deciding how data collection, analysis, and use are governed?

At a surveillance crossroads

For many reasons, we have reached a critical point for choices about surveillance. The fact that surveillance is ambivalent does not allow complacency with regard to any variety of surveillance operating today. Yet we should still insist that some surveillance is desirable and dependable. Many question surveillance capitalism. Governments capitulate all too easily to its siren songs and when they recognize mistakes or acknowledge overreach, they have limited legal or policy resources to rein it in. Others are understandably anxious about developments in AI, increasingly adopted to augment surveillance. But citizens questioning systems such as facial recognition in public streets can start a debate about its admissibility.

A common complaint is that platforms often undermine resources for solidarity and collective action. At the same time, if surveillance capitalism is ascendant, it will also be because consumers acquiesce to its short-term individual rewards while failing to take advantage of the internet's still existing potential for democratic responses and reshaping by digital citizens.

Some emerging trends might channel surveillance in some fresh ways. Many grass roots initiatives that struggle for openness, fairness, and data justice are growing. Digital rights are sought by responsible consumers, those concerned with precarious work, and human rights groups. At a more academic level, a 2017 Royal Society UK report suggests specific ways of seeking human flourishing in relation to big data: protect individual and collective rights; ensure that data trade-offs are transparent, understandable, and inclusive; seek good practices—learn from success and failure; and enhance democratic governance.

To take one example, where decolonizing steps are required to address the gross inequities between colonial powers and those treated as second-class citizens, special care is needed to ensure that personal data is handled appropriately, so that coercive conditions are not perpetuated digitally. The quest for data sovereignty for Indigenous peoples expresses the need to have rights over their own information and for others to obtain consent before collecting, using, or disclosing their data. But even these positive aspirations will be limited if we do not also see beyond them. Rights can be notoriously ambiguous and important virtues such as transparency are not ends in themselves.

Flourishing requires treating all with dignity and respect, the fostering of trusting relationships, not being satisfied with half-measures, and full communication. Transparency and democracy may be desirable, even essential, but they themselves are not 'ends'; they are pathways to accountability, trust, and the common good. And even trust does not exist on its own. It assumes the presence of *trustworthiness*, required of both individuals and institutions, the more so as some once-democratic societies turn towards authoritarianism.

Surveillance and an optics of hope

The confident offers of 'surveillance solutions' are countered today by pleas for privacy, freedom, fairness, and democratic regulation. But it is easy to set things up as a struggle between binary opposites. In the liquid conditions of the present, clear alternatives are highly unlikely to characterize any future development. Surveillance is not intrinsically antisocial or overreaching. Rather, the present conjunction of trends and events thrusts it further in that direction. It is also profoundly complex. So the important task is to encourage awareness of current trends and to invite reflection, discussion, and debate on what sorts of futures seem desirable, and the promotion of new modes of resistance and fresh initiatives designed to show how such hoped-for futures might be realized.

Not surprisingly, the way surveillance is seen—its *optics*—today is often dystopic. Some insist that surveillance is necessarily negative, always compromised with corporate greed or political power. While understandable, this cannot be the whole story. Such a bleak tale allows no space for the uses of personal data to enhance human existence, whether in healthcare, the urban environment, aid for refugees, or, yes even in security measures. As we have seen, however, it is the way that surveillance is calibrated, organized, and permitted to expand that generates adverse optics. Another way forward would be to envision and encourage an optics of hope.

Surveillance capitalism is a newly dominant social, economic, and political formation. But surveillance is seen here not only in terms of an operator perspective but also in terms of everyday participation. This, after all, is one factor that distinguishes surveillance capitalism. It is based on the unprecedented participation of those surveilled. And that *informed* participation can and does make a difference.

Much scepticism, indignation, and outrage about surveillance is not merely understandable but necessary. However, leaving things there is far from sufficient. Another aspect of the quest for a different surveillance world is to envision possible futures, desirable alternatives that can be sketched or even tried out in pilot form. New opportunities open up, including ones that take advantage of the same internet and social media potential that underlies surveillance capitalism.

What about platform cooperatives, for instance? They use digital means such as websites and apps to sell products but workers and users are co-owners who make decisions democratically. It is likely and desirable that radical alternatives will work in tandem with the efforts at resisting or eliminating aspects of contemporary surveillance, and reducing economic incentives for omnivorous data collection.

Ironically, and perversely, Bentham's panoptic plan proclaimed itself as echoing the 'eye of God'—his plan was epigraphed with words from a biblical song: 'Thou art about my path and my bed, and spiest out all my ways...' Yet the primary mode in which the biblical 'eye' watches is not behavioural control but relational care. Australian novelist Tim Winton hints at this in *That Eye, the Sky*, exploring multi-directional but pre-electronic surveillance, including a child's eye view. That eye is for the disadvantaged, discriminated against, driven to desperate measures. This is a far cry from many of today's surveillance systems, but it is an apt reminder that things can be different, that surveillance may operate out of other origins, other impulses.

To see past both the complacent assumption that surveillance is fundamentally serving the common good, and the anxious opposition to new technologies and surveillance practices that are deeply dysfunctional, divisive, and discriminatory, is to open our eyes to other possibilities. If 'human flourishing' is a priority, it calls for wisdom and the reassertion of human agency. Such potentials should never be discounted. Surveillance can see and be seen differently. An optics of hope is available.

References

Chapter 1: Living with surveillance

S. Zuboff, *The Age of Surveillance Capitalism* (New York: Profile Books, 2019).

Chapter 2: Visible lives: invisible watchers

D. Lyon, 'Surveillance', *Internet Policy Review*, 11/4 (2022), doi: 10.14763/2022.4.1673.

A. Mubi Brighenti, *Visibility in Social Theory and Social Research* (London: Palgrave, 2010).

C. Dandeker, *Surveillance Power and Modernity* (Cambridge: Polity, 1990).

O. Gandy, 'Statistical surveillance: Remote sensing in the digital age', in K. S. Ball, K. D. Haggerty, and D. Lyon (eds), *Routledge Handbook of Surveillance Studies* (London: Routledge, 2012).

R. V. Ericson and K. D. Haggerty (eds), *The New Politics of Surveillance and Visibility* (Toronto: University of Toronto Press, 2006).

J. C. Scott, *Seeing like a State* (New Haven: Yale, 1999).

G. Simmel, 'The Stranger', in D. Levine (ed.), *On Individuality and Social Forms* (Chicago: University of Chicago Press, 1971); originally published in German (Leipzig) in 1908.

M. Foucault, *Discipline and Punish: The Birth of the Prison* (New York: Random House, 1978; translation of *Surveiller et punir: Naissance de la prison*, Paris: Gallimard, 1975).

A. H. Sa'di, 'Colonialism and surveillance', in K. S. Ball,
K. D. Haggerty, and D. Lyon (eds), *Routledge Handbook of
Surveillance Studies* (London: Routledge, 2012).

A. Smith, 'Not seeing: State surveillance, settler colonialism and
gender violence', in R. Dubrofsky and Shoshana Amielle Magnet
(eds), *Feminist Surveillance Studies* (Durham, NC: Duke
University Press, 2015).

S. Zuboff, *In the Age of the Smart Machine* (New York: Basic, 1988).

G. T. Marx, *Undercover: Police Surveillance in America* (Cambridge,
Mass.: MIT, 1988).

D. Lyon, *Surveillance Society: Monitoring Everyday Life*
(Buckingham: Open UP, 2001).

S. Mann, J. Nolan, and B. Wellman, 'Sousveillance: Inventing and
using wearable computing devices for data collection in
surveillance environments', *Surveillance & Society*, 1/3
(2003) 331–55.

A. Marwick, 'The public domain: Surveillance in everyday life,'
Surveillance & Society, 9/4 (2012) 378–93.

D. Bigo, 'Diagonal mass surveillance: Gulliver versus the Lilliputians',
Open Democracy, 5 March 2014.

D. Lupton, *Data Selves* (Cambridge: Polity, 2019).

D. Lyon (ed.), *Surveillance as Social Sorting: Privacy, Risk and
Digital Discrimination* (London: Routledge, 2003).

Chapter 3: Surveillance technologies in context

C. Norris, 'There's no success like failure and failure's no success at all:
Some critical reflections on the global growth of camera
surveillance', in A. Doyle, R. Lippert, and D. Lyon (eds), *Eyes
Everywhere: The Global Growth of Camera Surveillance* (London:
Routledge, 2012).

R. Kitchin, 'Civil liberties *or* public health, or civil liberties *and* public
health: Using surveillance technologies to tackle the spread of
COVID-19', *Space & Polity*, 24/3 (2020) 362–81.

K. D. Haggerty and R. Ericson, 'The surveillant assemblage', *British
Journal of Sociology*, 51/4 (2000) 605–22.

G. Deleuze, 'Postscript on the societies of control', *October*, 59 (1992) 3–7.

J. Cheney-Lippold, *We are Data: Algorithms and the Making of our
Digital Selves* (New York: NYU Press, 2017).

N. Arteaga Botello, *Sociedad de la vigilancia en el sur global: Mirando
America Latina* (Mexico City: Miguel Angel Porrua, 2009).

M. Andrejevic and N. Selwyn, *Facial Recognition* (Cambridge: Polity, 2022).

J. Lauer, 'Surveillance history and the history of new media: An evidential paradigm', *New Media & Society*, 14/4 (2011) 566–82.

E. Black, *IBM and the Holocaust* (New York: Dialog, 2012). This edition revises and adds to the original 2001 publication.

Citizen Lab, *Communities at Risk: Targeted Digital Threats against Civil Society*, 2014. At <https://targetedthreats.net/>.

J. Thompson, 'Mediated interaction in the digital age', *Theory, Culture & Society*, 37/1 (2018) 3–28.

C. Calhoun, 'The infrastructure of modernity: Indirect social relationships, information technology and social integration', in H. Haferkamp and N. Smelser (eds), *Social Change and Modernity* (Berkeley: University of California Press, 1992).

T. Mathiesen, 'The viewer society: Michel Foucault's panopticon revisited', *Theoretical Criminology*, 1/2 (1997) 215–34.

L. Bridges, 'Infrastructural obfuscation: Unpacking the carceral logics of the Ring surveillant assemblage', *Information, Communication & Society*, 24/6 (2020) 830–49.

Chapter 4: Data-driven surveillance: new challenges

N. Srnicek, *Platform Capitalism* (Cambridge: Polity, 2016).

F. Pasquale, 'Two narratives of platform capitalism', *Yale Law & Policy Review*, 35 (2016) 309–19.

d. boyd and K. Crawford, 'Critical questions for big data', *Information, Communication & Society*, 15/5 (2012) 662–79.

J. van Dijck, 'Datafication, dataism and dataveillance: Big Data between scientific paradigm and ideology', *Surveillance & Society*, 12/2 (2014) 197–208.

R. Clarke, 'Information technology and dataveillance', *Communications of the ACM*, 31/5 (1988) 498–512.

S. Brayne, 'Big Data surveillance: The case of policing', *American Sociological Review*, 82/5 (2017) 977–1008.

C. J. Bennett and D. Lyon, 'Data-driven elections', *Internet Policy Review*, 8/4 (2019).

CDEI *Interim report: Review into bias in algorithmic decision-making*, Centre for Data Ethics and Innovation (UK Government) (2019). Available online.

E. Snowden, *Permanent Record* (New York: Metropolitan Books, 2019).

K. Weitzberg, M. Cheesman, and E. Schoemaker, 'Between surveillance and recognition: Rethinking digital identity in aid', *Big Data & Society*, 8/1 (2021), doi.org/10.1177/20539517211006744.

J. Lepore, *If Then: How One Data Company Invented the Future* (New York: Liveright, 2020).

V. Eubanks, *Automating Inequality: How High-Tech Tools Profile, Police and Punish the Poor* (New York: St Martin's Press, 2018).

A. Ollier-Malaterre, *Living with Digital Surveillance in China: Citizens' Narratives on Technology, Privacy and Governance* (London: Routledge, 2023).

Chapter 5: Surveillance culture: an everyday reality

A. Marwick, 'The public domain, surveillance in everyday life', *Surveillance & Society*, 9/4 (2012).

D. Trottier, *Social Media as Surveillance* (Aldershot: Ashgate, 2012).

D. Lyon, *The Culture of Surveillance* (Cambridge: Polity, 2018).

J. Finn, 'Seeing surveillantly: Surveillance as social practice', in A. Doyle, R. Lippert, and D. Lyon (eds), *Eyes Everywhere: The Global Growth of Camera Surveillance* (London: Routledge, 2012).

J. Penney, 'Chilling effects: Online surveillance and Wikipedia use', *Berkeley Technology Law Journal*, 31/1 (2016) 119–74.

H. Koskela, 'Webcams, TV shows and empowering exhibitionism', *Surveillance & Society*, 2/2–3 (2004) 199–215.

D. Harkin, A. Molnar, and E. Vowles, 'The commodification of mobile phone surveillance: An analysis of the consumer spyware industry', *Crime, Media & Culture*, 16/1 (2019) 33–60.

D. Trottier, 'Digital vigilantism as weaponisation of visibility', *Philosophy and Technology*, 30/1 (2017) 55–72.

L. Brandimarte, A. Aquisiti, and G. Lowenstein, 'Misplaced confidences: Privacy and the control paradox', *Social Psychological and Personality Science*, 4/3 (2012) 340–7.

J. Obar and A. Oeldorf-Hirsch, 'The biggest lie on the internet: Ignoring the privacy policies and terms of service policies of social networking services', *Information, Communication & Society*, 23/1 (2020) 128–47.

A. L. Young and A. Quan-Haase, 'Internet revelation and internet privacy concerns on social network sites', at <https://dl.acm.org/doi/pdf/10.1145/1556460.1556499> (2009).

P. Marks, *Imagining Surveillance: Eutopian and Dystopian Literature and Film* (Edinburgh: Edinburgh University Press, 2015).

J. McGrath, *Loving Big Brother: Surveillance Culture and Performance Space* (London: Routledge, 2004).

J. Kavenna, *Zed* (New York: Doubleday, 2019).

D. Eggers, *The Circle* (New York: Knopf, 2013).

D. Eggers, *The Every* (San Francisco: McSweenys, 2021).

K. S. Ball, 'Workplace surveillance: an overview', *Labor History*, 51/1 (2010) 87–106. A vital contribution to debates over surveillance in the workplace.

D. Murakami Wood and K. S. Ball, 'Brandscapes of control: Surveillance, marketing and the co-construction of subjectivity and space in neo-liberal capitalism', *Marketing Theory*, 13/1 (2014) 47–67.

M. de Certeau, *The Practice of Everyday Life* (Berkeley: University of California Press, 1984); originally published as, *L'Invention du quotidien: Arts de Faire* (Montréal: Gallimard, 1980).

Chapter 6: Questioning surveillance: critical probes

K. Breckenridge, 'Lineaments of biopower: the bureaucratic and technological paradoxes of Aadhaar', *South Asia: Journal of South Asian Studies*, 42/3 (2019) 606–11. Reflects on the special issue on Aadhaar.

R. Khera (ed.), *Dissent on Aadhaar: Big Data Meets Big Brother* (Hyderabad: Orient Blackswan, 2019).

UN Economic Commission for Africa, *Digital ID & Interoperability*. At <https://www.uneca.org/dite-for-africa/digitial-id-%26-interoperability/>.

M. Van Oort, 'The emotional labour of surveillance', *Critical Sociology*, 45/7–8 (2018) 1167–79.

S. Igo, *The Known Citizen: A History of Privacy in Modern America* (Cambridge, Mass.: Harvard University Press, 2018).

A. Puri, 'A theory of group privacy', *Cornell Journal of Law and Public Policy*, 30 (2021) 477–538.

J. A. Kroll, 'Facial Recognition', *ACM Tech Briefs* (2022). At <https://dl.acm.org/doi/pdf/10.1145/3520137/>.

E. Zureik et al. (eds), *The Globalization of Personal Data: International Comparisons* (Montreal and Kingston: McGill-Queen's University Press, 2010).

J. Cinnamon, 'Social injustice in surveillance capitalism', *Surveillance & Society*, 15/5 (2017) 609–25.

P. Regan, 'Privacy as a common good in the digital world', *Information, Communication & Society*, 3 (2004) 382–405.

V. Steeves, 'Reclaiming the social value of privacy', in V. Steeves, C. Lucock, and I. Kerr (eds), *Privacy, Identity and Anonymity in a Network World* (Toronto: Oxford University Press, 2008).

C. J. Bennett and J. Gilliom, Debate on Bennett's essay, 'In defence of privacy', *Surveillance & Society*, 8/4 (2011).

H. Nissenbaum, *Privacy in Context: Technology, Policy and the Integrity of Social Life* (Stanford, Calif.: Stanford University Press, 2009).

J. Cohen, *Configuring the Networked Self: Law, Code and the Play of Everyday Practice* (New Haven: Yale University Press, 2012).

P. Fussey and D. Murray, *Independent Report on the London Metropolitan Police Service's Trial of Live Facial Recognition Technology* (University of Essex: HRBDT, 2019).

C. O'Neill, *Weapons of Math Destruction: How Big Data Increases Inequality and Threatens Democracy* (New York: Crown, 2016).

V. Eubanks, *Automating Inequality* (New York: St Martin's Press, 2018).

R. Ericson and K. D. Haggerty, *Policing the Risk Society* (Toronto: University of Toronto Press, 1997).

E. Zureik, *Israel's Colonial Project in Palestine* (London: Routledge, 2016).

O. Gandy, *The Panoptic Sort: Political Economy of Personal Information* (Boulder, Colo.: Westview, 1993; new edition: New York: Oxford University Press, 2021).

C. Fuchs, 'Political economy and surveillance theory', *Critical Sociology*, 39/5 (2012) 671–87.

S. P. Gangadharan and J. Niklas, 'Decentering technology in discourse on discrimination', *Information, Communication & Society*, 22/7 (2019) 882–99.

K. Ball, 'Exposure: Exploring the subject of surveillance', *Information, Communication & Society*, 12/5 (2009) 639–57.

B. Harcourt, *Exposed: Desire and Disobedience in the Digital Age* (Cambridge, Mass.: Harvard, 2015).

S. Singh, and V. Steeves, 'The contested meanings of race and ethnicity in medical research', *Social Science Medicine*, 265 (November 2020).

L. Taylor, 'Exploitation as innovation: Research ethics and the governance of experimentation in the urban living lab', *Regional Studies* (November 2020).

Chapter 7: Encountering surveillance: what to do?

S. Browne, *Dark Matters: On the Surveillance of Blackness* (Durham, NC: Duke University Press, 2015).

G. Marx, 'A tack in the shoe: Neutralizing and resisting the new surveillance', *Journal of Social Issues*, 59/2 (2003).

M. Ogasawara, 'A tale of the colonial age, or the banner of new tyranny? National ID card systems in Japan', in D. Lyon and C. Bennett (eds), *Playing the Identity Card* (London: Routledge, 2008).

S. Davies, *Big Brother: Australia's Growing Web of Surveillance* (Sydney: Simon and Schuster, 1992).

J. Turow, *The Aisles Have Eyes: How Retailers Track your Shopping, Strip your Privacy and Define your Power* (New Haven: Yale University Press, 2017).

V. Arroyo and D. Leufer, 'Facial recognition on trial: Emotion and gender "detection" under scrutiny in Brazil', *AccessNow* (29 June 2020). At <https://www.accessnow.org/facial-recognition-on-trial-emotion-and-gender-detection-under-scrutiny-in-a-court-case-in-brazil/>.

C. J. Bennett, *The Privacy Advocates: Resisting the Spread of Surveillance* (Cambridge, Mass.: MIT, 2008).

E. Isin and E. Ruppert, *Becoming Digital Citizens* (London: Rowman and Littlefield, 2020).

C. J. Bennett et al. (eds), *Transparent Lives: Surveillance in Canada* (also available as *Vivre à nu: La surveillance au Canada*) (Edmonton: Athabasca University Press, 2014).

T. S. Eliot, *Collected Poems 1909–1962* (London: Faber & Faber, 1974) 159.

Royal Society and British Academy, *Data Management and Use: Governance in the 21st Century* (2019) (available online).

M. Foucault, *A History of Sexuality* (New York: Vintage, 1990).

M. de Certeau, *The Practice of Everyday Life* (Berkeley: University of California Press, 2011).

L. Taylor, 'What is data justice? The case for connecting digital rights and freedoms globally', *Big Data & Society* (July–December 2017) 1–14.

T. Winton, *That Eye, the Sky* (New York, Scribner, 1986).

Further reading

Surveillance & Society, <https://ojs.library.queensu.ca/index.php/
surveillance-and-society/> A key source of up-to-date surveillance
scholarship. The flagship journal of the international Surveillance
Studies Network. Other relevant journals include *Big Data &
Society*; *Security Dialogue*; *The Information Society*; *Information,
Communication & Society*; *International Political Sociology*; *New
Media & Society*; *Information Technology & Ethics*; *Internet
Policy Review*.

Early studies of surveillance

Scholars started to see surveillance as a specific and discrete area for
social science and public policy research as early as the 1970s, and
especially from the 1980s and 1990s.

C. Dandeker, *Surveillance Power and Modernity* (Cambridge:
Polity, 1990).

D. Flaherty, *Protecting Privacy in Surveillance* Societies (Chapel Hill,
NC: University of North Carolina Press, 1989).

M. Foucault, *Discipline and Punish: The Birth of the Prison* (New
York: Vintage, 1977).

O. Gandy, *The Panoptic Sort: A Political Economy of Information*
(Boulder, Colo.: Westview, 2021; revised edition of 1993).

D. Lyon, *The Electronic Eye: The Rise of Surveillance Society*
(Cambridge: Polity Press, 1994).

G. T. Marx, *Undercover: Police Surveillance in America* (Berkeley:
University of California Press, 1988).

J. Rule, *Private Lives and Public Surveillance* (London: Allen Lane, 1973).

S. Zuboff, *In the Age of the Smart Machine: The Future of Work and Power* (New York: Basic Books, 1988).

General

A selection of significant texts shows the range of perspectives, including communication studies, criminology, political economy, sociology, and urban studies.

M. Andrejevic *iSpy: Surveillance and Power in the Interactive Era* (Lawrence: University Press of Kansas, 2007).

J. Gilliom. *Overseers of the Poor: Surveillance Resistance and the Limits of Privacy* (Chicago: University of Chicago Press, 2001).

J. Gilliom and T. Monahan, *Supervision: An Introduction to the Surveillance Society* (Chicago: University of Chicago Press, 2020).

D. Lyon, *Surveillance Studies: An Overview* (Cambridge: Polity Press, 2007).

G. Marx, *Windows into the Soul: Surveillance in an Age of High Technology* (Chicago: University of Chicago Press, 2016).

R. M. Pallito, *Bargaining with the Machine: Technology, Surveillance and the Social Contract* (Lawrence: University of Kansas Press, 2020).

G. Sewell, *Surveillance: A Key Idea for Business and Society* (London: Routledge, 2021).

T. Strom, *Globalization and Surveillance* (London: Rowman & Littlefield, 2020).

History

The history of surveillance is a rapidly growing and fascinating sub-discipline.

K. Boersma, R. van Brakel, C. Fonio, and P. Wagenaar (eds), *Histories of State Surveillance in Europe and Beyond* (London: Routledge, 2016).

K. Breckenridge, *The Biometric State: The Global Politics of Identification and Surveillance in South Africa, 1850 to the Present* (Cambridge: Cambridge University Press, 2014).

R. Heynen and E. van der Meulen (eds), *Making Surveillance States: Transnational Histories* (Toronto: University of Toronto Press, 2019).

R. Jeffreys-Jones, *We Know All about You: The Story of Surveillance in Britain and America* (Oxford: Oxford University Press, 2017).

J. Lauer, *Creditworthy: A History of Consumer Surveillance and Financial Identity in America* (New York: Columbia University Press, 2017).

A. W. McCoy, *Policing America's Empire: The United States, The Philippines and the Rise of the Surveillance State* (Madison: University of Wisconsin Press, 2009).

J. Reeves, *Citizen Spies: The Long Rise of America's Surveillance Society* (New York: NYU Press, 2017).

Security and policing

Surveillance is commonly associated with security and policing, with which it has a long history.

L. Amoore, *The Politics of Possibility: Risk and Security Beyond Probability* (Durham, NC: Duke University Press, 2013).

D. Bigo, 'Security, surveillance, and democracy', in K. S. Ball, K. D. Haggerty, and D. Lyon (eds), *The Routledge Handbook of Surveillance Studies* (London: Routledge, 2012).

S. Brayne, *Predict and Surveil: Data, Discretion and the Future of Policing* (New York: Oxford University Press, 2022).

A. G. Ferguson, *The Rise of Big Data Policing: Surveillance, Race, and the Future of Law Enforcement* (New York: NYU Press, 2019).

S. Graham, *Cities Under Siege* (New York: Verso, 2010).

G. Greenwald, *No Place to Hide: Edward Snowden, the NSA and the US Surveillance State* (New York: Signal, 2014).

R. K. Lippert, K. Walby, I. Warren, and D. Palmer (eds), *National Security, Surveillance and Terror* (London: Palgrave Macmillan, 2016).

A. A. Magnet, *When Biometrics Fail: Gender, Race and the Technology of Identity* (Durham, NC: Duke University Press, 2011).

T. Monahan, *Surveillance in the Time of Insecurity* (New Brunswick: Rutgers University Press, 2010).

Social sorting and social inequality

Surveillance often reproduces and sharpens inequalities of many kinds.

S. Browne, *Dark Matters: On the Surveillance of Blackness* (Durham, NC: Duke University Press, 2015).

L. Arroyo Moliner and P. Frowde, 'Social sorting', in B. A. Arrigo (ed.), *The Sage Encyclopedia of Surveillance, Security and Privacy* (Thousand Oaks, Calif.: Sage Publishing, 2018).

R. E. Dubrofsky and S. A. Magnet (eds), *Feminist Surveillance Studies* (Durham, NC: Duke University Press, 2015).

O. Gandy Jnr, *The Panoptic Sort: A Political Economy of Personal Information* (2nd edition, New York: Oxford University Press, 2021).

R. Hall, *The Transparent Traveler: The Performance and Culture of Airport Security* (Durham, NC: Duke University Press, 2015).

R. Kitchin, *The Data Revolution* (London: Sage, 2014).

D. Lyon (ed.), *Surveillance as Social Sorting: Privacy, Risk and Digital Discrimination* (London: Routledge, 2003).

D. Lyon, *Pandemic Surveillance* (Cambridge: Polity, 2021).

S. U. Noble, *Algorithms of Oppression: How Search Engines Reinforce Racism* (New York: New York University Press, 2018).

E. van der Meulen and R. Heynen (eds), *Expanding the Gaze: Gender and the Politics of Surveillance* (Toronto: University of Toronto Press, 2016).

Technologies

A selection of studies of the contribution to surveillance of specific technologies. Today they form a digital web.

B. Ajana, *Governing through Biometrics: The Biopolitics of Identity* (London: Palgrave Macmillan, 2013).

R. Benjamin, *Race after Technology* (Cambridge: Polity Press, 2019).

J. Cheney-Lippold, *We are Data: Algorithms and the Making of our Digital Selves* (New York: New York University Press, 2017).

R. Clarke, 'Risks inherent in the digital surveillance economy: A research agenda', *Journal of Information Technology*, 34/1 (2019) 59–80.

A. Doyle, R. Lippert, and D. Lyon, *Eyes Everywhere: The Global Growth of Camera Surveillance* (London: Routledge, 2012).

K. Gates, *Our Biometric Future: Facial Recognition Technology and the Culture of Surveillance* (New York: NYU Press, 2011).

B. C. Newell, *Police Visibility: Privacy, Surveillance, and the False Promise of Body-Worn Cameras* (Oakland, Calif.: University of California Press, 2021).

F. Pasquale, *The Black Box Society: The Secret Algorithms that Control Money and Information* (Cambridge, Mass.: Harvard University Press, 2015).

G. D. Smith, *Opening the Black Box: The Work of Watching* (New York: Routledge, 2015).

Privacy

Much is written about privacy, traditionally a key area, especially for legal and policy research.

C. J. Bennett and C. D. Raab, *The Governance of Privacy: Policy Instruments in Global Perspective* (London: Routledge, 2017).

C. J. Bennett, *The Privacy Advocates: Resisting the Spread of Surveillance* (Cambridge, Mass.: MIT Press, 2010).

S. Igo, *The Known Citizen: A History of Privacy in Modern America* (Cambridge, Mass.: Harvard University Press, 2018).

H. Nissenbaum, *Privacy in Context: Technology, Policy and the Integrity of Social Life* (Stanford, Calif.: Stanford Law Books, 2009).

J. Rule, *Privacy in Peril: How We are Sacrificing a Fundamental Right in Exchange for Security and Convenience* (New York: Oxford University Press, 2007).

R. Wacks, *Privacy: A Very Short Introduction* (Oxford: Oxford University Press, 2010).

Politics and democracy

The interplay of political and economic power is a crucial theme in understanding surveillance.

K. S. Ball and L. Snider (eds), *The Surveillance–Industrial Complex: A Political Economy of Surveillance* (London: Routledge, 2013).

K. S. Ball and W. Webster, *Surveillance and Democracy in Europe* (London: Routledge, 2020).

J. Cohen, *Between Truth and Power: The Legal Constructions of Informational Capitalism* (New York: Oxford University Press, 2019).

C. Fuchs, 'Surveillance and Critical Theory', *Media and Communication*, 3/2 (2015).

K. D. Haggerty and M. Samatas (eds), *Surveillance and Democracy* (London: Routledge, 2010).

L. A. Viola and P. Laidler (eds), *Trust and Transparency in an Age of Surveillance* (London: Routledge, 2022).

Artistic, critical, and ethical viewpoints

L. Dencik, A. Hintz, J. Redden, and Emiliano Treré, 'Exploring data justice: Conceptions, applications and directions', *Information Communication and Society*, 22/7 (2019) 873–81.

K. D. Johnson, *Profiles and Plotlines: Data Surveillance in Twenty-First Century Literature* (Iowa City: University of Iowa Press, 2023).

K. Macnish, *The Ethics of Surveillance: An Introduction* (London: Routledge, 2017).

J. E. McGrath, *Loving Big Brother: Performance, Privacy and Surveillance Space* (New York: Routledge, 2004).

N. Mirzoeff, *The Right to Look: A Counterhistory of Visuality* (Durham, NC, and London: Duke University Press, 2011).

T. Monahan, *Crisis Vision: Race and the Cultural Production of Surveillance* (Durham, NC: Duke University Press, 2022).

E. Morrison, *Discipline and Desire: Surveillance Technologies in Performance* (Ann Arbor: University of Michigan Press, 2016).

D. Rosen and J. Santesso, *The Watchman in Pieces: Surveillance, Literature and Liberal Personhood* (New Haven: Yale University Press, 2013).

E. Stoddart, *The Common Gaze: Surveillance and the Common Good* (London: SCM Press, 2021).

Index

For the benefit of digital users, indexed terms that span two pages (e.g., 52–53) may, on occasion, appear on only one of those pages.

ADVERTISING

A Very Short Introduction

Winston Fletcher

The book contains a short history of advertising and an explanation of how the industry works, and how each of the parties (the advertisers , the media and the agencies) are involved. It considers the extensive spectrum of advertisers and their individual needs. It also looks at the financial side of advertising and asks how advertisers know if they have been successful, or whether the money they have spent has in fact been wasted. Fletcher concludes with a discussion about the controversial and unacceptable areas of advertising such as advertising products to children and advertising products such as cigarettes and alcohol. He also discusses the benefits of advertising and what the future may hold for the industry.

www.oup.com/vsi

ANTISEMITISM
A Very Short Introduction
Steven Beller

Antisemitism - a prejudice against or hatred of Jews - has been a chillingly persistent presence throughout the last millennium, culminating in the dark apogee of the Holocaust. This *Very Short Introduction* examines and untangles the various strands of antisemitism seen throughout history, from medieval religious conflict to 'new' antisemitism in the 21st century. Steven Beller reveals how the phenomenon grew as a political and ideological movement in the 19th century, how it reached it its dark apogee in the worst genocide in modern history - the Holocaust - and how antisemitism still persists around the world today.

www.oup.com/vsi

CITIZENSHIP
A Very Short Introduction
Richard Bellamy

Interest in citizenship has never been higher. But what does it
mean to be a citizen of a modern, complex community? Why is
citizenship important? Can we create citizenship, and can we
test for it? In this fascinating Very Short Introduction, Richard
Bellamy explores the answers to these questions and more in a
clear and accessible way. He approaches the subject from a
political perspective, to address the complexities behind the
major topical issues. Discussing the main models of citizenship,
exploring how ideas of citizenship have changed through time
from ancient Greece to the present, and examining notions of
rights and democracy, he reveals the irreducibly political nature
of citizenship today.

'Citizenship is a vast subject for a short introduction, but Richard
Bellamy has risen to the challenge with aplomb.'

Mark Garnett, TLS

www.oup.com/vsi

COMMUNISM
A Very Short Introduction
Leslie Holmes

The collapse of communism was one of the most defining moments of the twentieth century. At its peak, more than a third of the world's population had lived under communist power. What is communism? Where did the idea come from and what attracted people to it? What is the future for communism? This Very Short Introduction considers these questions and more in the search to explore and understand communism. Explaining the theory behind its ideology, and examining the history and mindset behind its political, economic and social structures, Leslie Holmes examines the highs and lows of communist power and its future in today's world.

Very readable and with its wealth of detail a most valuable reference book.

Gwyn Griffiths, Morning Star

www.oup.com/vsi

FREE SPEECH
A Very Short Introduction
Nigel Warburton

'I disapprove of what you say, but I will defend to the death
your right to say it' This slogan, attributed to Voltaire, is frequently
quoted by defenders of free speech. Yet it is rare to find anyone
prepared to defend all expression in every circumstance,
especially if the views expressed incite violence. So where do
the limits lie? What is the real value of free speech? Here, Nigel
Warburton offers a concise guide to important questions facing
modern society about the value and limits of free speech:
Where should a civilized society draw the line? Should we be free
to offend other people's religion? Are there good grounds for
censoring pornography? Has the Internet changed everything?
This Very Short Introduction is a thought-provoking, accessible,
and up-to-date examination of the liberal assumption that free
speech is worth preserving at any cost.

'The genius of Nigel Warburton's *Free Speech* lies not only in
its extraordinary clarity and incisiveness. Just as important is the
way Warburton addresses freedom of speech - and attempts to
stifle it - as an issue for the 21st century. More than ever, we need
this book.'

Denis Dutton, University of Canterbury, New Zealand

www.oup.com/vsi

FUNDAMENTALISM
A Very Short Introduction
Malise Ruthven

Malise Ruthven tackles the polemic and stereotypes surrounding this complex phenomenon - one that eludes him today, a conclusion impossible to ignore since the events in New York on September 11 2001. But what does 'fundamentalism' really mean? Since it was coined by American Protestant evangelicals in the 1920s, the use of the term 'fundamentalist' has expanded to include a diverse range of radical conservatives and ideological purists, not all religious. Ruthven investigates fundamentalism's historical, social, religious, political, and ideological roots, and tackles the polemic and stereotypes surrounding this complex phenomenon - one that eludes simple definition, yet urgently needs to be understood.

'...powerful stuff...this book is perceptive and important.'

Observer

www.oup.com/vsi

HUMAN RIGHTS
A Very Short Introduction
Andrew Clapham

An appeal to human rights in the face of injustice can be a heartfelt and morally justified demand for some, while for others it remains merely an empty slogan. Taking an international perspective and focusing on highly topical issues such as torture, arbitrary detention, privacy, health and discrimination, this *Very Short Introduction* will help readers to understand for themselves the controversies and complexities behind this vitally relevant issue. Looking at the philosophical justification for rights, the historical origins of human rights and how they are formed in law, Andrew Clapham explains what our human rights actually are, what they might be, and where the human rights movement is heading.

www.oup.com/vsi

NEOLIBERALISM
A Very Short Introduction
Manfred B. Steger & Ravi K. Roy

Anchored in the principles of the free-market economics, 'neoliberalism' has been associated with such different political leaders as Ronald Reagan, Margaret Thatcher, Bill Clinton, Tony Blair, Augusto Pinochet, and Junichiro Koizumi.So is neoliberalism doomed or will it regain its former glory? Will reform-minded G-20 leaders embark on a genuine new course or try to claw their way back to the neoliberal glory days of the Roaring Nineties? Is there a viable alternative to neoliberalism? Exploring the origins, core claims, and considerable variations of neoliberalism, this Very Short Introduction offers a concise and accessible introduction to one of the most debated 'isms' of our time.

'This book is a timely and relevant contribution to this urgent contemporary topic.'

I. K. Gujral, Former Prime Minister of India

PRIVACY
A Very Short Introduction
Raymond Wacks

Professor Raymond Wacks is a leading international expert on privacy. For more than three decades he has published numerous books and articles on this controversial subject. Privacy is a fundamental value that is under attack from several quarters. Electronic surveillance, biometrics, CCTV, ID cards, RFID codes, online security, the monitoring of employees, the uses and misuses of DNA, - to name but a few - all raise fundamental questions about our right to privacy. This *Very Short Introduction* also analyzes the tension between free speech and privacy generated by intrusive journalism, photography, and gratuitous disclosures by the media of the private lives of celebrities. Professor Wacks concludes this stimulating introduction by considering the future of privacy in our society.

www.oup.com/vsi

PUBLIC HEALTH
A Very Short Introduction
Virginia Berridge

Public health is a term much used in the media, by health professionals, and by activists. But what do we mean when we speak about 'public health'?

In this *Very Short Introduction* Virginia Berridge explores the areas which fall under the remit of public health, and explains how the individual histories of different countries have come to cause great differences in the perception of the role and responsibilities of public health organisations. Drawing on a wide range of international examples, Berridge demonstrates the central role of history to understanding the amorphous nature of public health today.

www.oup.com/vsi

TERRORISM
A Very Short Introduction
Charles Townshend

What is terrorism? Is terrorism crime or war? What can we do to stop it?

In this *Very Short Introduction*, Charles Townshend unravels the questions at the heart of the problem of terrorism. He details the impact and consequences of terrorism through exploration into recent terror attacks including those in Brussels, Paris, Nice, and Rouen. Looking at recent terrorism, Townshend discusses the emergence of ISIS, the significant rise in individual suicide, and the issue of 'cyberterror'. As well as answering central questions in regard to terrorism, he also details counterterrorist measures used by authorities, ranging from control orders to drone strikes.

www.oup.com/vsi